XD
8376

EAST SUSSEX

SHELF MARK	Y 388 ·34233
COPY No.	01556925
DATE 3/97	AU ST 6/02

Kaleidoscope of
CHAR-A-BANCS
And Coaches

(20401) HY, ZZ

By Stan Lockwood

PUBLISHED BY
MARSHALL HARRIS & BALDWIN LTD
17 AIR STREET LONDON W1

THE AUTHOR

ONE-TIME car salesman, semi-professional comedian, booking clerk and driving instructor Stan Lockwood has had a varied career, including a long spell in the agricultural machinery business, a five-year stint as a GPO operator and several years as sales director with a Ford main dealership.

He joined the Central London Coach Station in 1930 and in the course of his activities met many of the coaching personalities of that era, using his camera to the full to record those exciting days. An ex-Desert Rat tank commander, he was mobilised as a Territorial just before the outbreak of war and took part in the great tank battles of 1941/2 in the Libyan Desert. Blown up in an enemy minefield at Alamein, he was in at the kill when Tripoli fell three months later and was one of the first tanks to reach the outskirts of Tunis. Then, attached to the American Fifth Army, Stan was in the Salerno landings in Southern Italy and again he and his crew had to 'bale out' in a skirmish just north of Naples, returning to England for D-Day.

He was Mentioned in Despatches whilst in Normandy and, when hostilities ceased, became an instructor in tank driving and tactics in Belgium and Germany, but did not return to the coaching scene when finally handed his demob suit.

For the past 12 years or so he successfully ran his own business in children's wear, and although now retired to sunny Devon, he spends the summers in the industry he started in 50 years ago - booking holidaymakers on Wallace Arnold excursions. Unfortunately, most of Stan Lockwood's collection of pre-war photographs and timetables went missing whilst he was overseas, but his recollections of the pre-war pioneering coaching days are as strong as ever, and he is a regular writer for our *ALBUMS*.

The author, in schoolboy kit, poses at the wheel on a 1923 charabanc excursion from Palmers Green in North London to Hampton Court.

Pictured in 1931 this AEC Regal of Queen Line heads northwards after leaving Barnet.

FOREWORD

GREAT BRITAIN is a fortunate country, indeed, in having a very highly developed motor coach industry. From the lavishly equipped executive coach with its conference tables and cocktail bars, right down through the spectrum to the humble racecourse excursion, all classes and tastes are catered for. The country is criss-crossed with regular express routes, and for the more adventuresome there are even scheduled services to other countries and other continents. The private and state-owned sectors between them provide a host of facilities which are probably second to none in the world.

Today's coaching system is the result of a progressive development over many years. In the early days enterprise was paramount and

competition was rife. Things are more settled today, but even now the entrepreneur still has ample scope for his talents, particularly in the field of private hire, and forthcoming parliamentary legislation is likely to bring renewed vigour to the industry.

The initial framing of our great coach network makes a fascinating story as we trace the stages of development from the crude, open-air charabanc on its solid tyres through to the modern luxury vehicle. The years from 1925 to 1930 were of particular significance in that they saw the build-up of regular long distance coach services reach its peak, much to the great discomfiture of the complacent railway companies whose finances felt the pinch and who retaliated by purchasing shares for themselves in large chunks of the coach industry. The efforts of the early pioneers which, together with those of the many small body building firms and chassis manufacturers of the day, combined

to produce a most comfortable and economical form of passenger transport, are outlined in this volume. Endeavours have been made, by means of picture and story, to give an informal insight into the evolvement from charabanc to super coach, but the reader will appreciate that only the highlights of this eventful history can be recounted.

My grateful thanks go to the many friends in the industry who have assisted in the supply of information and the loan of photographs, and particularly to Ken Blacker, who has contributed additional text and illustrations; also to Geoff Lumb and Chris Taylor for proofreading. A special 'thank you' goes also to Ken Brown of Devon General, Reg Hele and Gordon Hoare of Wallace Arnold, Fred Darke of National/Ribble, and Ken Bateman of Grey Green. To those old established operators who have not been mentioned within these pages I can only say 'there's always a next time'.

THE PIONEERS

Speedy reliable travel to all parts of the country in executive comfort is now taken for granted, but spare a thought for those exciting, pioneering days right at the start of the present century when motor coach touring was at its very beginning.

AT first the motorised public vehicle was slow coming into its own, and the early tentative steps with fragile little wagonettes often brought no financial reward to their entrepreneurs, merely countless hours of work and worry. Roads were, by and large, in poor condition and shook the primitive, wooden-wheeled vehicles to pieces. The early machinery was unreliable and erratic, and skilled mechanics were very hard to come by. Drivers accustomed to the gentle nature of horses found the intricacies of gear changing and other idiosyncrasies of the mechanism hard to master, and they had to learn to deal with breakdowns on the road. To make matters worse, the motor vehicle was not

always well-received, in fact, great hositility to it was shown by some town councils. Small wonder that horse-drawn carriages remained in use on seaside and country excursions right up to World War I, although in diminishing numbers as the reliability and general acceptance of motor charabancs increased. Despite all hazards, the motor charabanc developed and prospered. (*Char-a-bancs*, as it was often spelled, was the name most commonly used for motor coaches in the early days; it derived from the French *carriage with benches*). There was certainly no lack of patronage. It became the poor man's transport and opened up completely new vistas for many in the

industrial areas, giving countless people their first glimpse of the sea and of parts of the countryside that they would never otherwise have known.

1 At the turn of the century, when trips by public motor vehicle were in the very first stages of infancy, most of the enterprising men who tried their luck in the new industry chose to purchase little wagonettes seating no more than ten or twelve. One of the earliest pioneers was T H Barton, who started running this two-year-old 6hp Daimler in Mablethorpe in 1900. It is seen, a year later, working at Weston-super-Mare, whence it occasionally made trips to such beauty spots as Cheddar, Wells and Glastonbury. The vehicle, which had been bought in a dismantled state for £75, was very reliable for its time. From these tiny beginnings grew the huge Nottinghamshire-based Barton concern which we know today.

2 Motoring in the very early days was uncomfortable, uncertain and -- above all -- expensive. For the latter reason the early wagonettes soon died out as they were simply not large enough to permit operation at a profit. The pioneering operators turned instead to much larger vehicles suitable for carrying either passenger or lorry bodies -- and often both, according to the prevailing demand. By 1905, when this tiered charabanc was produced, the shape of things to come was beginning to be clearer. This machine carried as many as 23 passengers accommodated in two bucket seats on either side of the gangway with a let-down seat in the gangway itself. Luggage was carried in a box under the floor. The manufacturer was the Lancashire Steam Motor Company, which was destined, two years later, to become Leyland Motors Ltd.

3 The major railway companies were quick to grasp the depth of the potential threat to their revenue from motor vehicles, and some of them decided to fight the new enemy on its own ground by buying charabancs of their own. The North Eastern Railway was one. Many of the more reliable chassis available in the very early years were of Continental manufacture -- mainly from France and Germany -- but in this instance the company purchased a 30hp Saurer, an import from Switzerland, through the Motor Car Emporium Ltd. Unlike the vehicle in the previous photograph this one is completely open to the elements and there is no centre gangway. The cross bench seats have to be reached by means of a small portable ladder; no mean feat for lady passengers in the long dresses of the time.

4 Maudslay built this vehicle for Scottish Motor Traction in 1906, one of a number, some of which had double deck bodies whilst others were charabancs such as this. The company's first chief engineer, Caithness man William J Thompson, drew up a stringent set of requirements which he expected his buses to attain, one of which was that they should be able to reach 3 mph on a 1 in 3 gradient, and only Maudslay met these requirements in full. The choice proved a wise one, as all gave several years good service.

This "Commer Car" Char-à-banc has been running continuously since 1910. The owner, Mr. Charlie Clarke, Retford, says :—"To my way of thinking 'Commer Cars' are the best in the world."

5   One of the most successful early chassis was the Milnes-Daimler, a product of the old established tram manufacturer, G F Milnes & Co Ltd, and built to the designs of the German Daimler company incorporating German-built engines. On this 1907 vehicle, supplied to Jones Brothers of Aberystwyth, the chain drive favoured by many early manufacturers has given way to a propellor shaft. The rather exotic looking body is not, strictly speaking, a charabanc as it has fixed side railings and a centre gangway, entry to the passenger saloon being achieved via a small staircase at the rear. The flimsy canvas top looks very insecure, and it is a matter of conjecture how long it would have stood up to a hefty pounding from the rough Welsh roads of the time.

6   Charlie Clark of Retford purchased this Commer Car in 1910 and got good service from it. Commer realised earlier than many of their contemporaries that refinements were needed for passenger work that need not be applied to lorries. They also tackled the problem that defeated so many would-be drivers, the gear change, and standardised on an effective preselector mechanism well in advance of Daimler's more famous efforts in this field in the nineteeen thirties. The gearbox was designed by a London garage owner, C M Linley and the control lever for it was mounted on the steering column just below the steering wheel. Reliable home-produced chassis, such as the Commer Car, had almost eliminated the foreign competition by this time -- for a while at least. The charabanc body is all on one level, the tiered vehicle having now had its day, and the even sized wheels front and rear give a much more modern appearance.

7   A further refinement on this well-laden 1912 Durham Churchill is the fitting of individual doors to each row of seats, a useful safety feature which took a surprisingly long time to become standard. The canvas hood, neatly stowed away at the rear for dry weather travel, has also made its appearance. These early 'boneshakers', with wooden wheels, solid tyres and precious little springing, gave a woefully rough ride on potholed country lanes or on cobblestoned city streets. But such was the novelty of the vehicles in this dawning of the motor age that there was seldom any difficulty in achieving a full load.

8 The pioneering spirit brought some real peculiarities in its wake, not least of which was this strange stagecoach-like creation, one of a pair built in 1911 by the Thames Ironworks, Shipbuilding & Engineering Co Ltd and incorporating massive 4ft 6ins diameter rear wheels. Thames was just one of many concerns who turned to motor construction as their traditional markets in other fields dwindled away. The company was one of the earliest to construct a chassis especially for bus work and it pioneered the six cylinder engine years before it became a standard feature. It also became involved in bus operation through a subsidiary, Motor Coaches Ltd. Despite being to the forefront of vehicle design Thames had acute money problems, and though it made strenuous efforts to survive it was forced into liquidation in December 1912. Fortunately, one of these strange stagecoach vehicles still survives as a preservation piece.

9 Another curiosity was this 3 ton Foden steamer with removable charabanc body belonging to Holt Brothers of Rochdale and photographed in 1912. Although covered by an ornate awning, the passengers had no side screens to protect them from the elements, or from the smuts from the chimney. Though

interchangeable charabanc and lorry bodies were commonplace, few went to the extreme of making demountable charabanc bodies for steam wagons. Little did the owners visualise that, fifty years on under the title of Yelloway

Motor Services Ltd, their pioneering company would be operating fast motorway schedules between their home town of Rochdale and London, covering the journey between Manchester and London in five hours dead.

10 In various parts of the country pioneers were initiating trips to their own particular local beauty spots. Visitors to Whitby, for example, had the opportunity of a 30 mile excursion across the wild North Yorkshire moors to the villages of Glaisdale and Lealholm. Photographed in 1913, this Leyland carried two drivers, and presumably in the unfortunate event of a breakdown one driver would stay with the passengers whilst the other would trudge the lonely moorland roads to obtain assistance. Judging by the large peat stack outside the cottage in the background, a harsh winter is expected! Note the extra large acetylene lamp positioned in front of the Leyland's radiator. The charabanc body has now been further refined to provide a neat, unbroken line of doors and intermediate panels along each side; indeed only a windscreen now remains to be added before it reaches its final form.

11 Visitors to the fine Welsh resort of Llandudno had the choice of trips run by several local owners and one pioneering concern was the Llandudno Automobile Touring Co Ltd. The mountainous nature of the surrounding beauty spots taxed the capabilities of the early charabancs to the full, but in this early scene a Dennis has successfully carried its passengers into the wild grandeur of Snowdonia. Rather unusually it is not carrying any lights, and notice the four feet of hollow tube which connects the squeeze bulb by the side of the driver to the horn alongside the bonnet.

12 Southend-on-Sea, that Mecca for Cockney day trippers, could boast two highly competitive and efficient charabanc operators in 1913. The Southend-on-Sea Charabanc Co Ltd had several Dennises in its Royal Blue fleet, whilst Holmes & Smith Ltd ran Thornycrofts under the title of Royal Red. One of the latter's 20-seaters is seen backing out of its proprietor's cramped yard preparatory to starting off on a half-day trip. Despite some lubrication troubles with the big end bearings, the company's four Thornycrofts successfully maintained a whole series of excursions ranging from South Benfleet and Thundersley for 2/- [10p] to Yarmouth Races for 36/- [£1.80]. A particularly popular run was to Canterbury via the Tilbury ferry.

13 The motor vehicle was naturally slower in reaching the more remote and undeveloped parts of the nation, but by the outbreak of war even the smallest and most remote of the outlying islands had experienced the snorts, bangs and rattles of the motoring age. The Hebridean island of Islay, best renowned for its malt whisky distilleries, played host to its first commercial motor vehicle in 1914. A fixed-roof Commer Car charabanc, it was brought across on the MacBrayne steamer by the enterprising proprietor of the Islay Motor Company, James Kean. Note the gentleman in the front passenger seat playing the bagpipes.

14 The immediate pre-war era saw a resurgence of interest by foreign chassis builders in the British market. To the forefront was Berna, but much to its consternation a direct rival, British Berna Motor Lorries Ltd, was set up in Guildford in 1914 and went energetically into competition with the parent Swiss concern. A good example of the British Berna output is this 35-40hp charabanc, a 35-seater and the second of a pair purchased by the Express Motor Company of 35 Oxford Road, Belfast. It was used for a single brief season prior to the war on the tourist trade between Bangor and Donaghadee, Co Down.

15 Very *alfresco*! An informal 1914 gathering at Tarporley Races in Cheshire. The Daimler on the left was owned by the New Brighton Motor Coach Co Ltd, whilst the picnic party in the centre have made the trip from Bury. The New Brighton concern was registered in May 1914 although operations had commenced the previous year. Daily excursions were initiated through the Wirral Peninsula, and in later days 3-day extended tours of Wales and 7 days to Devon and Cornwall were regularly conducted When a Receiver was appointed in December 1928 the company owned eleven Daimle 28-seater coaches.

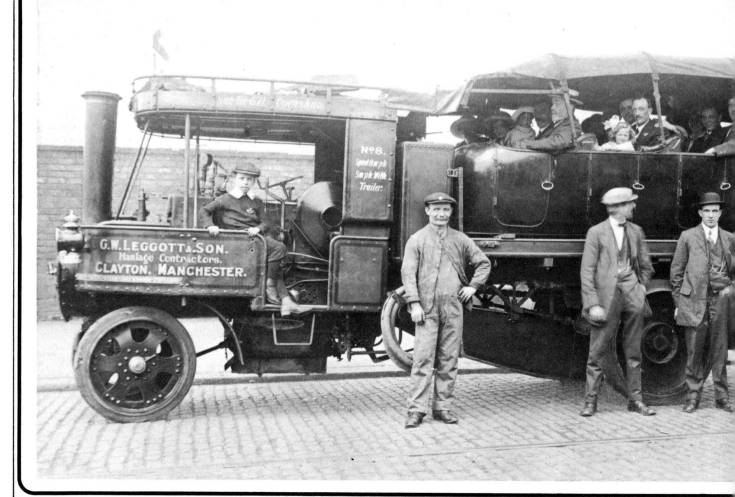

16   War came to Britain on 4th August 1914. The whole motorbus industry suffered an immediate setback as skilled drivers and mechanics enlisted. At the same time huge quantities of the best vehicles were commandeered, with or without their bodies, for military use. Charabanc operation almost came to halt for the duration. Under war conditions it proved hard enough to maintain essential bus services, so the continuance of pleasure operations was out of the question. However, not everyone was completely deterred. G W Leggott & Son of Clayton, Manchester, clearly reckoned that, with wartime fuel problems, any charabanc was better than none, as instanced by this fine old coal-fired Mann wagon with a charabanc body placed precariously on top. Pictured in 1917.

17   To conserve precious wartime petrol stocks many vehicles were converted to run on domestic gas. Several manufacturers competed for the sale of gas installations and this one was the Lyon-Spencer supplied by Ernest Lyon Ltd of 91 New Bond Street. Most systems, such as this one, relied on an inflatable bag positioned on the vehicle's roof and they operated reasonably satisfactorily. It was often claimed that the cost of operating on gas was approximately one third that of petrol, but the range was strictly limited. The charabanc illustrated here has been impressed for war service with the Royal Navy.

LURE OF THE OPEN ROAD

**The Armistice was signed on 11th November 1918, and it was a signal for everybody -- except the multitudes who never came back -- to resume a normal life. But the balmy Edwardian days were gone for ever and, in a land that should have been fit for heroes, many found it a struggle to get by.
The coaching industry was in tatters and had to pick itself up and start all over again, and it lost no time in doing so.**

THERE was an immediate clamour for the resumption of coach excursions and tours, and the demand was insatiable. Most of the population had, by force of circumstances, been obliged to stay at home for four years, or else they had been away from their families whilst serving in the Forces. Now it was time to start to enjoy life again, and people felt the urge to travel. Coaching's boom was aided by the inability of the railways to adapt quickly to peacetime conditions. Operators benefited almost immediately from the influx of a huge number of war surplus chassis, large numbers of which were sold through Slough Lorries & Components Ltd, who wooed prospective buyers with slogans like *Come to Slough in Bargain Time*. Many were American built, and scores of ex-servicemen, with their gratuities to spend, bought cheap reconditioned chassis from Slough and entered the field of charabanc operation with them. Many of these chassis, with exotic names like Peerless and Pierce-Arrow, Bethlehem and Hawkeye, were soon to be seen bearing the post-war travelling public to pastures new.

18 The Isle of Wight has always offered quaint and picturesque scenery for the holiday maker, and these natural attractions were made more accessible by the coming of the motor vehicle. Surrounded by the charming thatched-roof houses, the gossiping pedestrians seem completely oblivious of the 28-seater Leyland passing through Shanklin village. Pictured in the immediate post-war years the rebuilt ex-RAF 4 ton chassis is minus one electric headlamp but carries two acetylene side lights. Leyland had been particularly wise in purchasing in bulk all the war surplus Leylands that they could lay their hands on. These were then thoroughly overhauled before being re-sold. In this way Leyland protected their good name whilst other manufacturers, notably Daimler, had to live down the bad name caused by poorly overhauled war surplus chassis from Slough, some of which were so unreliable as to bring their new owners close to the point of ruin.

19 The post-war demand for new charabanc bodies was enormous, and all over the country, in workshops big and small, craftsmen laboured long hours to meet the demand. In many primitive and often ill-equipped workshops, former wheelwrights and joiners adapted their skills to producing the odd charabanc body or two in what became something of a thriving cottage industry, whilst at the other end of the scale a few large manufacturers turned out several bodies a week on early twenties versions of the mass production line. One such manufacturer was the Bristol Tramways & Carriage Co Ltd in whose works no fewer than seventeen bodies can be seen in various stages of construction in this September 1920 view. The majority are 29-seaters for fitting to the company's own very excellent Bristol 4 ton chassis which found many enthusiastic customers.

20   Home based manufacturers went through a very bad time due to the influx of so many cheap, ex-war service chassis, and many smaller firms went to the wall during the nineteen twenties. Even some of the larger ones, such as Daimler, Dennis and Leyland went through a lean time. A typical Daimler of 1920 manufacture features prominently in this traffic jam at Epsom Downs where cars and taxis mingle with the popular charabancs, all heading for a parking space by the race track. Having unloaded its passengers, the solid tyred 22-seater of Samuelson's is followed by a couple of Leylands of Waterloo Belle, one with its hood raised, and all patiently waiting their turn to move forward. Through the maze of fumes and dust an open top double decker can be seen in the queue. The Daimler sports new fangled electric lighting equipment -- acetylene lamps were the order of the day only a short while earlier -- and, as windscreen wipers were not yet in vogue, the driver had to peer through the half-opening windshield when it was raining.

21 United Service Transport Co Ltd of Clapham Road, SW9 -- later to become one of London's biggest fleet operators -- owned this beautifully painted Daimler example of the early 1920 era. Clambering up the steps and through the individual nearside doors was sometimes a problem as not all vehicles carried a portable ladder to assist in entry and exit. In sudden rain showers passengers tried to assist the driver in raising the hood from its folded position at the rear but, occasionally, it was a case of 'too many cooks' and those occupying the front seats were wet through before the hood was in place. Canvas sidescreens with small celluloid windows were clipped to the side whilst the hood front was held down by leather straps attached to brackets on the two front mudguards. By 1930, with bodybuilders vying with each other to produce the ultimate in comfort and styling, people tended to look back on the charabanc, which had served them so well, as a cumbersome monstrosity.

22 The ubiquitous Ford Model T one tonner, with its classic and unique transmission system and great ease of manoeuvrability, endowed itself to very many operators. Moreover, it was cheap to buy and thus came within the financial capability of many who could not afford a larger vehicle when commencing their coach-owning career. Many were subjected to chassis conversions of one sort or another to increase their carrying capacity from about twelve people up to a more economical level. One of the deficiencies of the charabanc is illustrated in this 1920 view of a Model T operated by Mills & Seddon of Bolton; there was virtually nowhere to store baggage. The problem in this case has been solved by tying various items with string to each side of the bonnet. Judging by the petrol can lying in front of the vehicle, the stop may have been an involuntary one and not purely for the convenience of the photographer.

[Left and far left]
23 & 24 The use of dual-purpose bodies -- lorries in the week and charabancs at weekends -- persisted from pre-war days and did not finally die out until the middle twenties. The feverish activity in countless ill-lit sheds all over the country on Friday evenings to convert a workaday truck into a presentable passenger coach can be easily imagined, and several enterprising coachbuilding concerns marketed specially designed kits for the purpose. One such conversion set was the Magnet body marketed in 1921 by Ellison & Smith Ltd of Gatley, Manchester. As shown in the accompanying illustrations, the dash and windscreen, wings and running boards were fixed items, but the remainder could be quickly removed to provide either a 12-seat charabanc or a one-ton van or flat truck as in the case of this vehicle for W Heald of Normanton. The charabanc body was sturdily built in hard wood and panelled in steel. The seats were rexine covered and the usual waterproof hood was provided for wet days.

25 Whoops-a-daisy! The lady looks a trifle apprehensive as she receives a helping hand from the driver of this solid tyred 'chara' awaiting its passengers in London's Holborn district. The bowler-hatted gentleman takes the precaution of donning his overcoat before climbing the three steps to the individual rows of seats -- it could be very breezy when on the move. The easily accessible vertical door catches are located on the top of each door -- and the smartly attired chauffeur is complete with leather gloves. The plain painted side panels suggest that many owners had not yet appreciated the full publicity value obtained by displaying their name or service, an omission remedied to the extreme a few years later.

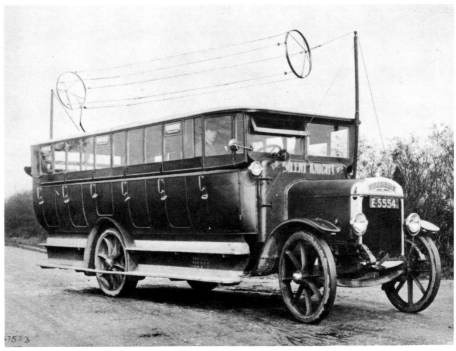

[Below left]

26 'Public motoring is not now only a matter of half-day beanfeasts and short distance joy rides as it used to be at one time. It has developed into a high class travel facility that appeals to all classes and pockets alike, and the standard of vehicle has risen accordingly'. So stated a press correspondent in 1920, but it is difficult to see how he justified his claim that the standard had risen significantly since pre-war years as the solid tyred, open-to-the-elements charabanc was still the norm. A conscious effort to provide a smoother than usual ride was, however, made by Tilling-Stevens with its petrol electric system which, free of conventional gearchanging, produced what the manufacturer described as the 'jerkless journey'. In this early post-war Hampshire scene, a TS3A model 23-seater is seen in the maroon and black livery of Birch Brothers Ltd, a London-based concern with its origins way back in horse bus days.

27 Who said that vehicle radio is comparatively new? This fine old 1921 40hp Thornycroft charabanc must have been one of the very first public service vehicles to be fitted with a wireless set. An unsightly aerial to modern eyes, but no doubt reasonably effective. With the author having nostalgic childhood memories of the family crystal set, and having to keep quiet whilst Father, with bated breath, tried to find the right spot with the 'cat's whisker', presumably reception through earphones was only possible when the vehicle was stationary. Any jolting on the move would upset the delicate poising of the all-important 'cat's whisker'. This early 28-seater, which appears to have been well ahead of its time in having a detachable roof, was owned by Silent Knight Motor Services of Chasetown, Staffs.

28 The delights of Torbay attracted a particularly large outing in 1921 when members of the Bolton Co-operative Society made the long rail journey south, to be met by a vast fleet of coaches. Local operators mustered their resources to transport the party to their hotels and then undertook sightseeing trips to beauty spots in the district. Some of the vehicles required for the visitors are pictured in Lucius Street, Torquay, lining up outside the booking office which is still used today for Wallace Arnold excursions. The sixteen charabancs are in various shapes and sizes, but the leading pair are both small capacity, pneumatic tyred Fiats. These, and many other overseas makes, were on the British market throughout the twenties, providing a stimulus to home manufacturers to march with the times faster than they might otherwise have done.

29 Another popular import from abroad was the Italian-built Lancia which was renowned for its speed. This 18-seater of Court Coaches, on an excursion from Torquay, carries two spare wheels and sports a pair of magnificent carriage lamps. It was the 'done thing' to be photographed on a coach trip and drivers invariably had certain private arrangements. On tours to Clovelly, Dartmoor, Plymouth, etc, coaches would stop at Torre station where a photographer would have his tripod and watch-the-birdie camera in position. On the return journey vehicles would again stop whilst the enterprising photographer sold the developed picture to the eager passengers. The drivers would each receive a free photo for themselves plus a shilling gratuity. Court Coaches was the last of the small operators in the Torbay area when the company -- Court Garages [Torquay] Ltd -- sold its business on 1st October 1966 to the Grey Cars offshoot of Devon General.

30 Still on the subject of coaches imported from abroad, one of the less well remembered was the Gotfredson which was not, as its name might suggest, of Scandinavian origin, but which came from Canada. It really was, as this 1924 advertisement says, a good climber and it was fast, too. Thanks to an energetic sales drive it sold in steady numbers for two or three years, particularly in the eastern counties. There is certainly no false modesty here in the claim that the Gotfredson was the best chassis in the world, though nowadays such a claim would no doubt raise a few eyebrows amongst those administering the Trades Description Act!

[Top right]

31 Some charabanc operators were notoriously aggressive in their advertising and marketing policies, and as a result their growth was rapid. One such was Timpson's Silver Service based in London and Hastings which, in addition to its coaching activities, also ran profitable bus services in both centres. Timpsons were able to cater for very large party bookings without the need to subcontract work to their competitors, and in this view eight of their Karriers are seen, with their drivers, parked on the green outside *The Elephant's Head Inn* at Hook Green, near Lamberhurst. The Timpson name lasted prominently for very many years, though latterly it has sunk within the anonymity of the National Bus Company, who use its old Catford headquarters as the base for National Travel [London] Ltd.

32 Even as late as 1926 a charabanc trip through the beautiful Scottish highlands could be a great adventure, such was the state of many of the principal highways. Solid tyres and potholed roads were a combination that only the hardiest of travellers could really have relished. The twisty road leading up to the infamous Devil's Elbow between Blairgowrie and Braemar was, at 2199 ft above sea level, the highest public road in Great Britain. It was normally largely deserted, but on this occasion motorists heading for the Braemar Gathering have created a Highland version of a traffic jam. A passengerless Bristol charabanc stands in the foreground, but whether its stop was intentional or not we shall never know.

33 The most famous of all hill climbs was reckoned, by the industry at large, to be the very testing Porlock Hill in Somerset. Good publicity was always ensured for any charabanc capable of surmounting it. When Bristol brought out its new 2 tonner in 1924 it gave the model an unusually thorough testing by running a number of vehicles fully loaded up to approximately 17,000 miles each over Devon roads, including the ascent and descent of Porlock Hill several times each day. One of the prototypes, a pneumatic tyred 20-seater, is seen being tested on the sharp incline. The full fronted design is a comparatively new innovation for a touring vehicle, and it remained rare when combined with the old charabanc body whose days were now numbered.

[Right]

35 A reminder of a bygone age with charabancs in profusion. An occasion when local operators supplied vehicles for a mass private hire excursion also gave an opportunity for an unusual picture. Thirty-seven charabancs are viewed from 160ft up when a trip around Dartmoor was organised for members of the Ancient Order of Foresters. The fleet is about to set off from the Guildhall Square, Plymouth, and included in it are two empty units. Could it be that, in the event of a breakdown, passengers could transfer to the spare vehicles?

34 Elderly passengers could not always get the knack -- nor indeed did they always have the strength -- to raise one leg high enough to ensure a firm footing on the second step and then hoist themselves up, and this picture shows the difficulties experienced at times. It wasn't too easy climbing down either. Small wonder, then, that the charabanc quickly faded out of popularity once the saloon coach came firmly on the scene. This Harrington-bodied Southdown Tilling-Stevens petrol electric of 1925 was a late example of new charabanc production, but such was the speed of obsolescence that the body was removed about 1927 and replaced by a double decker for stage carriage operation. Note the one oil lamp at the rear of the vehicle, although the wiring to it suggests that it was converted to electrical operation.

THE MOTOR COACH GROWS UP

The resumption of coaching activity after the end of World War I was, as we have already seen,
accomplished almost entirely with vehicles little changed in style and comfort
from those which had pioneered the motoring age two decades earlier.

The open-to-the-elements, high sided charabanc with its hard to reach cross-bench seats was still generally regarded as good enough for the working class masses at which the coaching market was generally aimed, and attempts to improve the breed were at first slow to catch on.

However, change was inevitable; people were quickly becoming more discerning and operators who persisted in clinging to the old charabanc concept were destined for failure. Modernisation, though slow at first, quickly gained in momentum, and such was the eventual speed of progress that the ten years from 1920 to 1930 saw the greatest strides in motor coach development of all time.

36 The all-weather was the stepping stone from charabanc to fully enclosed saloon coach, and a motley assortment can be seen lined up at the start of a private outing. The sleek vehicle at the head of the column has an exceptionally long body with a big overhang whilst the Lorna Doone coach has a fitted framework to take the canvas hood and also sports a small luggage rack on the fixed roof rear end. The third in the convoy is an older vehicle of the 'chara' variety but now on pneumatics, which has carriage lamps but is minus headlights, although the lamp brackets are in position. The following vehicle is also high bodied but with fixed side windows and fitted with hood framework, whilst the fifth is a small 20-seater with a section of fixed roof at front and rear leaving the centre portion open. This coach also boasts a luggage rack. The whole scene -- set in Lambeth Road, SE1 near the junction with Kennington Road -- is watched with great interest by the inhabitants of the flats above the shops.

37 One of the passenger transport industry's great 'characters', the late H Orme White, claimed to have pioneered the centre gangway coach as a popular alternative to the traditional cross-bench charabanc. The high body line, the open top, and the hard-to-handle folding hood are still there, but the breakaway from the charabanc concept has begun. Passengers take their seats on this 1920 Palladium which basks in the Cleethorpes sunshine before setting off on a tour of the local beauty spots. Palladium was a London based manufacturer who, though they tried hard, failed to avoid the bankruptcy which also overtook other small chassis builders in the mid-twenties.

38 The London General Omnibus Co Ltd was another concern to favour the saloon coach at an early stage. Its 1921 batch of 23-seater private hire coaches on chassis supplied by AEC, an LGOC associate company, had only one entrance. However, the internal layout was not as simple as might have been expected, passengers having to thread their way between alternating rows of two and four seats. At the inspiration of Mr Gage, superintendent of General's coach factory, the folding hood was unusually placed at the front instead of at the rear, giving the coach a somewhat bare and unfinished appearance when viewed from the back. It was claimed that this arrangement gave the driver better visibility when reversing, but it has not been recorded what drivers thought of having the hood cumbersomely folded up in front of them.

39 Luxury all round. Not only a fixed roof but pneumatic tyres, too! Both are seen on this saloon-bodied Daimler, photographed near Maidenhead on a demonstration run in November 1920, and were advanced features for their day. The general use of pneumatic tyres for a vehicle of this size was still five or six years away. The vehicle looks ultra modern for its time, and although fixed side windows are yet to make their appearance, the shape of things to come is already apparent.

40 The best of both worlds in one coach. Short Brothers were backing their horses both ways in 1923 when they built this charabanc-cum-saloon coach on a Lancia Tetraiota chassis. The front end is built in open charabanc style whilst the saloon behind it provides enclosed, all-weather comfort for half the passengers. Curiosities of this sort were rare, but they served to illustrate the conflicting lines of thought with which the coaching industry was criss-crossed at the time.

41 A seaside operator prepares for the season. A pair of Westcliff-on-Sea Royal Red Daimler all-weathers -- saloon coaches with folding back roofs -- stand at the operator's Pier Hill garage in Southend-on-Sea. The white walls of the pneumatic tyres add an air of smartness in line with the image created by the smart uniforms of the drivers. A vast range of half and whole day excursions is offered, and the company was well into the field of all-inclusive extended tours as proclaimed on the garage canopy; a sphere in which it excelled for many years. Their claim to have 'the finest fleet of coaches in the country -- experienced and careful chauffeurs' was not far from the truth.

42 London's Hotel Victoria is the background setting for a small line-up of all-weather Halleys engaged on charter work and owned by Keith & Boyle [London] Ltd, operators of Orange Luxury Coaches. Apart from seasonal services to the coast, the company operated sightseeing and afternoon tours in and around London. They had a close working relationship with The District Messenger & Theatre Ticket Co Ltd, and by appointing this organisation as agents, Orange Luxury obtained a fair amount of overseas visitors' business. In 1928, with at least three other concerns working into the capital with similar names -- Orange Brothers of Bedlington, Orange Coaches of Chatham and Orange Coaches [Dover] Ltd, Orange Luxury issued an advertisement stating that they had no connection with any firms running under a like title.

43 Motor coach touring took on new dimensions in the nineteen twenties as more and more operators launched out into this lucrative form of summer operation. Organisational and operational problems were gradually overcome, and hotels in many resorts became geared up to deal with 'package' coach parties. And for countless people the tours opened up new vistas, people who had never travelled far afield or stayed at hotels in the whole of their lives. Some incredible bargains were there for the taking, such as this tantalising, all-inclusive Timpson's six day tour to Devon for a mere 9½ guineas [£9.97½] offered in 1927.

44 The days of the all-weather were strictly numbered in 1928, but nevertheless even major coachbuilders such as Duple were still busy constructing vehicles of this type. One such item of Hendon output was this substantial looking 26-seater mounted on a McCurd chassis and intended as a demonstrator for this small, struggling chassis manufacturer. The dual entrance body layout had now become popular, even on quite small vehicles, and a useful feature was a Barwatt patent one-man hood

TIMPSON'S SUPERB SIX-DAY HOLIDAY TOUR
TO ILFRACOMBE AND NORTH DEVON.

AT the request of hundreds of our clients a Superb Tour, embracing North Devon, has been arranged.

The inclusive fare of 9½ guineas allows for First-Class Hotel accommodation and all gratuities (except to the chauffeur.)

A reasonable amount of luggage will be allowed.

The Coaches used have been specially built for long distance tours, and are of the bucket seat type, low, excellently sprung, fast and reliable

All passengers are assured that Messrs. Timpson's will arrange all details to ensure a perfect Six-Day Holiday.

The Tour will start from Catford every Sunday (commencing June 12th).

TIME TABLE—SUNDAY.

Leave Catford Garage	8.30 a.m.
Leave Charing Cross Embankment ... ... (Outside Underground Station)	9. 0 ,,
Arrive " White Hart Hotel," Salisbury, for Lunch	1. 0 p.m.
Arrive " County Hotel," Taunton, for Tea	5. 0 ,,
Arrive " Osborn Hotel," Ilfracombe, (Late Dinner)	8.30 ,,

MONDAY.—A day at Ilfracombe. Breakfast, Lunch, Tea and Dinner at the Osborne Hotel, Ilfracombe.

TUESDAY. —A Coach Trip to Lynton and Lynmouth, staying **5** hours to view " Watersmeet " and surroundings. Breakfast, *al fresco* Lunch and Dinner supplied by Osborne Hotel.

WEDNESDAY.—A Days' Tour to the ancient towns of " Clovelly " and " Westward Ho." Breakfast, *al fresco* Lunch and Dinner, supplied by Osborne Hotel.

THURSDAY.—Breakfast and Lunch at the Hotel, followed with a Coach Trip to the " Hunters' Inn," embracing wonderful scenery, returning to the Hotel for Dinner.

FRIDAY.—Early Breakfast at Hotel, depart at 8 a.m. for Cheddar (Lunch at Cliff Hotel). Free admission and conducted tour of Cox's Stallactite Caves. Then *via* the gorgeous Cheddar Gorge, Shepton Mallet, and on to Hungerford for Tea. Continuing *via* Reading, Wokingham, Ascot and Kingston, arriving home about 9.30 p.m.

mechanically operated by means of a detachable handle at the front end of the roof. The easy-to-work canvas hood was a great improvement over the unwieldy specimens that had been in use for some years, but it came too late to save the all-weather concept as solidly built roofs, some with sliding centre sections, were now being developed.

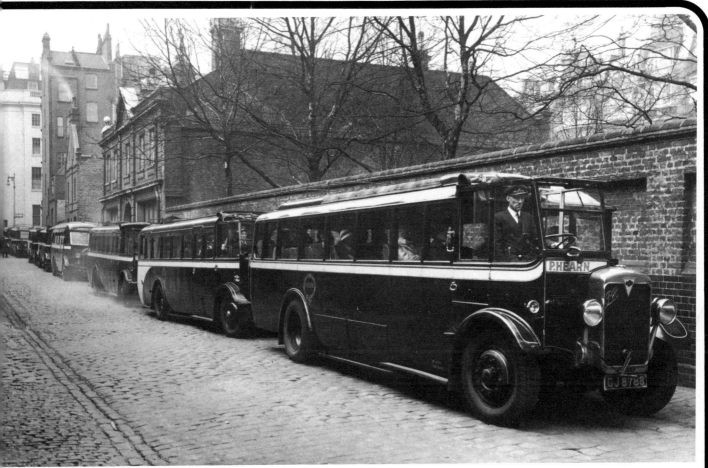

45 A considerable amount of private hire work was undertaken by London fleet owners on behalf of Thomas Cook & Son, Frames Tours and other travel organisations, transporting large numbers of tourists from railway stations to hotels, on London sightseeing trips and other excursions. 'Patsy' Hearn -- as he was familiarly known -- of Gray's Inn Road, WC1, ran a successful fleet catering specifically for this type of business. No regular coastal services were operated except that for a very short period he worked a route to and from Aylesbury under the name of The Atlas Coach. The AEC Reliances in this picture taken in the 1930s had a form of sunshine roof, inasmuch as the canvas top could be rolled back as far as the luggage rack, and the driver's cab was likewise equipped with a roll-back top. The fourth vehicle -- an early Dennis Lancet -- has been sub-hired from Empress Motors of Cambridge Heath and is rather more modern than the Hearn contingent.

46 Derby Day 1931, and traffic piles up as always en route for Epsom. The motive power of the very front vehicle may lack the grace of a Derby winner, but some classics of the late twenties and early thirties coaching scene are to be found following it. Foremost is a fairly rare Laffly -- an import from France -- followed by an impressively solid looking Albion with its canvas hood firmly buttoned down as if in anticipation of wet weather. Next comes a forward control Gilford, an unknown all-weather, and a Leyland service bus, with double deckers bringing up the rear. From the earliest motor coaching days the Derby has always been --and still is -- one of the biggest draws in the private hire calendar.

47 Prominent amongst the several London suburban companies operating seasonal services to the east and south coasts, Valliant Direct Coaches Ltd -- originated by Mr G R Valli of Acton Lane, W4 -- had their own departure station at Ealing. Although in post-war times Valliant faded sadly away, in pre-war days it was a strength to be reckoned with as this departure scene at Ealing shows. In this busy Saturday view, AEC Regals, Gilfords and Leyland Tigers, three of the most popular coach chassis on the road 1931, are equally represented. Gone completely are the old all-weather machines, and all of these are hard topped vehicles with sliding sunshine roofs in the latest idiom. Most have long since been scrapped but, miraculously, the Weymann semi-fabric-bodied Gilford on the left still survives in preservation.

---

48 Robert Barr was a young Leeds-based motor coach pioneer who was early in the field of extended tours to Devon, Scotland and Wales. By 1925 he owned 25 vehicles and then, on the eve of the General Strike in 1926, the partnership of Wallace Cunningham and Arnold Crowe was acquired -- hence the name of Wallace Arnold Tours. The demand for day excursions to the Dales, Lakes and the Coast, together with touring holidays, was growing all the time, and 1933 saw the company's first Continental tour -- to Germany. To publicise their activities, Wallace Arnold despatched this 1930 Leyland Tiger to London on a 'show-the-flag' sales promotion drive. The author duly photographed this sturdy looking 26-seater one murky January morning in 1932 outside the headquarters of the Central London Coaching Station at Argyle House, King's Cross, before escorting the coach on visits to various travel agents. Coaches quickly became obsolete in the nineteen thirties, and in 1937 a new, streamlined Duple body replaced the original on this machine. It was further modernised in 1949 by Wallace Arnold subsidiary Wilkes & Meade, and did not finally depart from the fleet until 1951.

[Far right]
49 This 1932 AEC Regal with Duple bodywork was the first coach in Blackpool to be fitted with radio -- the aerial wires running round the outside of the roof. It was purchased by J Abbott & Sons [Blackpool] Ltd to start their 1932 Fleetwood-Manchester express service worked jointly with Lansdowne Motors -- a concern who had started operations in the early 1920s. Abbotts have grown from the time they acquired Stevenson Brothers in 1931 together with two Crabtree-bodied Reos, to the present fleet of twenty coaches, all AECs, with the majority Plaxton-bodied. Over the years Abbotts, with their well-known motif 'The Jolly Abbott', have expanded by buying Richard Blackhurst [Blackpool] Ltd in 1950, with extended tour licences and some seven or eight vehicles, Lansdowne Motors in 1955 and Enterprise Motors [Blackpool] Ltd in 1976.

RAILWAYS BEWARE

**From the rapid growth of local tours and private hire, it was but a short step to the setting-up
of frequent, long distance coach services. Up to 1925 such services had not really got underway on any regular basis
although a few pioneering operators had already experimented with short distance schedules.**

SOUTHDOWN had worked a daily London service from Brighton during the 1919 railway strike, and in the same year Royal Blue of Bournemouth had run trips to the metropolis which had proved so successful that a twice weekly service was introduced in the following year. Orange Coaches of Chatham was another pioneer who claimed they were the originators of the Gillingham-London run in 1921. But the really big day came on 10th February 1925 when Greyhound Motors Ltd of St Augustine's Place, Bristol -- a local bus and charabanc operator -- started the country's first all year round daily express schedule between that city and London, carrying passengers between inter-mediate towns en route as well as between terminals. There were, of course, the pessimistic Jonahs who

questioned the wisdom of such a step, but their warnings quickly proved unfounded and the venture highly successful. Greyhound undercut the railway fare on the Great Western by a considerable margin, and while the four main line railways looked on askance, Greyhound's lead was taken up by other operators at a remarkable pace. By the end of the decade, express services radiated out of London to all points of the compass, like the spokes of a wheel, and passengers to some particularly popular destinations were treated to a bewildering variety of competing services, often at cut-throat fares, and there were many useful cross-country connections that had sprung up, too.

By 1929, for example, seven companies were running between Manchester and London, eight

between Liverpool and London, whilst six connected Great Yarmouth with the capital.

50 Greyhound's pioneering London-Bristol service started with a pair of solid tyred Dennises but pneumatic tyred ADCs were soon added. In 1927 five 'super de luxe buffet coaches' enhanced the standard of service still further. Based on ADC 416A chassis, their Strachan & Brown bodies contained only 26 red antique leather covered seats. Eighteen were accommodated in the front saloon, with a further eight in the smoking compartment at the rear. In the centre there was a small buffet on one side and a lavatory on the other. Initial London-Bristol journey time was 8 hours with a departure from Prince Street, Bristol, at 9am running via Chippenham, and another at 11am routed by way of Devizes, also returning from Hammersmith Broadway at the same times. Conductors were carried and through passengers were charged £1 for the return fare. Ramsay MacDonald, then an MP and later to become Prime Minister for the second time, was amongst the VIP party who travelled on the first journey from London on the day following commencement of the service, 11th February. The wheels by Esco are non-standard.

The lack of an overall licensing system made this state of affairs possible, but it was all too good to last. The popularity of coach travel was badly affecting rail revenue and the four main line companies protested bitterly that the public were using road vehicles instead of travelling by train -- naughty public for daring to choose their own method of travel! Since the end of the stage coach, the railways had had a near monopoly

51 The long distance passenger road service was starting to come into its own when, in November 1926, George Readings, proprietor of Black & White Coaches of Charlton Kings, Cheltenham, inaugurated a daily service to London, leaving Cheltenham at 8.45am. The service travelled by way of Northleach, Burford

and Witney for a 15 minute halt at Oxford, and thence via Henley, Maidenhead and Slough to London. The return vehicle left at 2pm, rather an early start, but the idea was to reach Oxford before dark because it was thought that passengers would not care to travel long distances at night. Initially, the London terminus was fixed at West Kensington District Railway station but it was soon decided that Hammersmith Broadway was more suitable, and by 1928 Black & White Motorways Ltd [registered in April of that year] had opened their own office and terminal point at 15A Hammersmith Bridge Road. The service commenced with 6 cylinder Reo Pullmans with 21-seater all-weather bodies by London Lorries, one of which is seen terminating at West Kensington.

---

52 Several operators found the 15ft 4ins wheelbase Studebaker 'Big Six' suitable for medium distance routes with the chassis lending itself admirably to the fitment of high class

bodywork such as this well proportioned Strachan & Brown 20-seater supplied to Rural England Motor Coaches Ltd in 1927. The two boat-type ventilators installed just in front of the windscreen are an unusual fitment, and the exterior colour scheme consisting of imitation grained walnut panelling below the waistline, chrome uppers and a black roof, with mouldings picked out in gold, was highly effective. Rural England was started in December 1928 by two former London 'pirate' busmen, George Finlay and Edward Hoiland. When J H Watts' more powerful Red & White began express services in April 1929 they met Rural England at Gloucester and also painted their express service vehicles in Rural England livery. In 1929 J H Watts began operating his own services and Rural England were out on a limb and began operating to South Wales on their own with not enough vehicles, agents, etc. The battle which ensued saw Rural England forced into liquidation early in 1930.

Travel to Bristol—Weston-s.-Mare—Torquay
by the "Morning Star" Express Motor Coaches.
(The Most Luxurious of all Road Services.)

DAILY SERVICE

—

LONDON
SLOUGH
MAIDENHEAD
READING
NEWBURY
MARLBOROUGH
CHIPPENHAM
BATH
MARSHFIELD
BRISTOL
WESTON-SUPER-MARE
BRIDGWATER
TAUNTON
WELLINGTON
EXETER
TEIGNMOUTH
DAWLISH
TORQUAY
(for PAIGNTON)

HEAD OFFICE :
55, Lawrence Hill,
Bristol.
'Phone 5464.

—

HEAD LONDON AGENT :
Charles Rickards,
Ltd., 12, Spring St.,
Paddington, W.2.
Paddington 5686.

—

TORQUAY AGENTS :
Lamboll & Ingham,
Ruby Cars,
The Strand,
Torquay.
'Phone 2626.

Seats must be Booked in Advance.

53 The pioneering Greyhound company had competition on the A4 in 1928 when Royal Blue of Bournemouth started a London-Bristol-Weston super Mare service with a departure at 10.15am from both termini using 6 cylinder ADCs. At the same time the 1923 established firm of E Jones & Sons Ltd of Bristol appeared on the London road with their twice daily Morning Star schedule via Reading, the service increasing in 1929 with two additional departures running by way of Swindon and Oxford. The single fare was 10/- [50p] but another 6d [2½p] was payable if one travelled via Oxford. Morning Star were already operating between Bristol and Torquay, so by linking the two services into a through route, they offered intending passengers to and from the Torbay area a choice of three completely different itineraries by three operators. Although Morning Star's through Torquay journey was scheduled at 11½ hours against the 9 hours of Royal Blue via Salisbury and the 11 hours of Modern Travel via Bournemouth, the fares were the same at £1 single and 35/- [£1.75] return. The Bristol firm's advertising of 1928 illustrated one of its modern Leyland Lionesses, but in 1932 the express services of Morning Star were acquired by Greyhound.

53A A particularly enterprising innovation dating from mid-1927 was Russell's Restaurant Car service on the London-Folkestone run, operated by Robert Russell, proprietor of the Hawkinge Motor Company of Folkestone who had started local bus operations in 1923. The vehicle bought for the commencement of the service was this Phoenix-bodied Gilford 6 cylinder machine, painted in an attractive buff livery with wide, olive green waistband. The 20 semi-armchair seats were upholstered in hide with the inner sides finished in padded antique leather, whilst a hinged table folded into the back of each row of seats. Underneath each seat was a drawer containing a rug. The saloon ceiling was covered in a beautifully moulded washable lincrusta with five frosted lamps partially inserted in the roof and, underfoot, the floor was covered with brown cork lino. As a finishing touch the windows were fitted with brown casement curtains. A telescopic ladder for reaching the 20-suitcase capacity roof rack was clipped under the front of the chassis.

---

with hardly any competition in the long distance field until the express coach came along. From 1929 the four railway companies started investing heavily in the various territorial bus undertakings controlled by the combine groups, thus getting a substantial stake in bus and coach operations. The financial agreement between the rail and road giants was spurred on by the creation of the Royal Commission on Transport in 1929, whose findings were to form the basis of the 1930 Road Traffic Act.

The Road Traffic Act brought regulation and stability, and a rapid diminution in the number of express service operators. Destinies were shaped by the Act when the big guns of the giants were ranged against the slim and limited resources of the small independents, resulting in long, wordy and expensive battles in the traffic courts. Some survived, but many gave up the unequal struggle, and the field was left to the large territorial undertakings with just a smattering of independent companies, the decisions of the Commissioners making it well nigh impossible for newcomers to enter the arena of express services.

53B The rear end of the Russell Gilford held the most attention, and a notable feature was the folding gate which could be pulled across the entrance, allowing the main door to be left open whilst the vehicle was in motion so that the back part of the saloon could serve as a smoking compartment. Hot meals could be prepared in a specially fitted oven, a yacht-type primus stove being an essential part of the equipment in supplying two burners, one for the oven and another for the kettle. In this view, a steward is seen carrying a tea tray from the kitchen into the saloon. His stock of utensils included twenty complete sets of crockery, wine and liqueur glasses, water jugs and coffee pots, the water supply for cooking and washing up being supplied from a 40 gallon copper tank mounted under the rear of the body. The coach was also equipped with a lavatory, the entrance to which can be seen just to the right of the entrance gate.

54 Craftsmen at the Hendon factory of Duple in the autumn of 1928 would have wept tears of anguish had they known that this coach on which they were lavishing all the care and skills of their trade was soon to be a write-off. Built to the order of G Askew & Sons of Loughton, Essex, for their London-Plymouth service, the chassis selected was a rare Gilford 6 wheeler. The beautifully appointed saloon seated 33 persons with upholstery in brown hide, finished at the edges with round headed oxydised nails. Each passenger was provided with a rug rail, footrest and built-in ashtray, and other equipment included a machine on the front bulkhead dispensing cigarettes, matches and chocolate. The driver's cab had curtains for the side windows instead of glass panes and a roof which slid back into the saloon. Fitted with a 6 cylinder American Wisconsin engine, the vehicle was extremely fast, being capable of attaining speeds well in excess of 50 mph, and it was this power that contributed to the disaster which befell the 6 wheeler on the A30 at Fenny Bridges in Devon. Travelling at high speed, it jumped the humpback bridge over the River Otter, left the road, and crashed into a line of trees, resulting in a number of casualties.

55 As the long distance coach gained in popularity, a number of on-street terminal points were established in Central London, much to the disquiet of the Metropolitan Police, who were unhappy about the traffic congestion which resulted. This scene, taken one winter afternoon in the late 1920s outside the Underground station on the Victoria Embankment at Charing Cross, shows that coach travel was not confined to the summer months. More and more people were discovering this new economical method of transport. On the extreme left can be seen the tail end of a Weald of Kent coach waiting to leave for Rye, behind which is a Dennis of Westminster Coaching Services Ltd, bound for Bury St Edmunds. In the centre is an all-weather Lancia with raised hood, followed by other vehicles waiting to load. It is interesting to recall that a suggestion was made in 1927 that a 10 mph speed limit should be imposed on this stretch of the Victoria Embankment, but the then Minister of Transport, in concurrence with the Commissioner of Police, objected on general traffic grounds and quite rightly maintained that the imposition of such a limit would be ineffective.

56 The joy of traffic-free motoring. A driver's paradise on the A31 approaching Ringwood, with just a watchful eye to be kept on the grazing New Forest ponies at the side of the road. Shamrock & Rambler's 9am London to Bournemouth service is being worked by a 26-seater Daimler parlour coach, one of twenty such models included in the company's thirty strong fleet. By 1928 Shamrock & Rambler were operating twice daily between the two centres, and the following year, with some eight companies providing intense competition on this popular route, fares were reduced to 10/- [50p] single and 15/- [75p] return. At the same time the frequency was increased to four return journeys a day. In 1935 Keith & Boyle [London] Ltd, owners of Orange Luxury Coaches, obtained a financial stake in the company, the Bournemouth-London express operations of both operators becoming a joint service.

57 The Merseyside Touring Co Ltd of 28 Chapel Street, Liverpool, was a comparative latecomer to the ranks of those on the London road. Formed in August 1929, the company's Liverpool office at 30 Islington had previously acted as terminal control agents for the London-based Claremont Luxury Coaches working via Oxford, Birmingham and Chester, until the Merseyside concern started its own service to the capital. A slightly indirect route was chosen to attract intermediate passengers and served Lichfield, Coventry, Rugby and Northampton, and they also developed long distance services from Liverpool to Scarborough, Great Yarmouth, Weston-super-Mare, Torquay, Bournemouth, etc. In company with other Lancashire operators, Merseyside carried a large number of parties from surrounding towns to the Grand National at Aintree, one of the few events of the year when owners quoted inclusive fares varying from 25/- [£1.25] to 30/- [£1.50] which covered travel to and from the course, hot soup on arrival, 6-course luncheon served on the coaches, tea and admission charge. This view shows two Merseyside vehicles at Blackpool in April 1930, a Massey-bodied Tilling-Stevens and a Bristol. Two months later the firm came under Ribble control.

58 The years of 1928 and 1929 saw the build-up of express routes reach its peak and it was at this period that Majestic Saloon Coach Tours of 9 Oxford Road, Manchester, joined in the London run. Soon to become Majestic Express Motors Ltd, the company worked day and night services between the two cities, travelling by day via Birmingham, Warwick and Oxford, with the overnight schedule going by way of Birmingham, Towcester and St Albans. Initially, three 4 cylinder Crossley Eagles were put on the road. They were fitted with full fronted Spicer bodies -- very advanced styling then -- and the appearance of the coach head-on gave it rather a determined and aggressive look. The low roof line of the cab, slightly extending over the windscreen, found favour with drivers on the southbound run in helping to reduce sun glare to a minimum. The vehicles were equipped with the usual curtains and lavatory, but this latter facility was omitted when a repeat order for Eagles was placed. A year or so later, AEC Regals were introduced into the fleet. When the service first commenced, the southern terminus was the London Terminal Station, with calls at 317 Regent Street and the Central London Station, but by 1934 Majestic Express had joined the London Coastal combine and was working out of the new Victoria Coach Station.

59 Varied indeed were the fleet names adopted by new companies opening up yet more routes, and none more imaginative than Palanquin -- closed carriage of the East. Palanquin Coaches Ltd started a London-Manchester service in late 1928 and, by selecting a most interesting road by way of Bedford, Kettering, Leicester, Derby, Matlock and Buxton, gave would-be travellers a fourth choice of route between the two cities. It was sometimes the practice for owners to launch new services in a blaze of publicity by engaging a West End star or some other personality to break a bottle of champagne over the vehicle's radiator, with press cameras clicking and movie cameras whirring. The resultant advertising in the national daily and evening papers continued to bring home to the public the full impact that coaching was having in this country. Pictured is a smart fawn and brown Dodson-bodied Leyland Tiger, duly garlanded, after its christening ceremony at Bush House, Aldwych. An AA badge is prominently displayed in case of need.

60 The intensity of long distance coaching competition found its greatest fulfilment on the Great North Road which, magnet like, lured many operators in a cut-and-thrust operation. It was all started by Orange Brothers of Market Place, Bedlington, Northumberland, who inaugurated their 273 mile Newcastle-London service in the summer of 1927. Initially, the service ran twice weekly in each direction but it soon developed into a daily run with departures from both ends at 8am, giving an advertised journey time of 12 hours. With their home base some 12 miles or so north of Tyneside, a further 23 miles was added to the route by leaving the Bedlington garage at 6.30am and taking the coastal road via Blyth, Whitley Bay, Tynemouth and North Shields en route to the main departure point at Newcastle's Haymarket, attracting useful additional business from these highly populated catchment areas. Early, normal control Gilfords started this long run, and in the severe winter of 1927 they met hazards as they negotiated the snow-covered A1 and male passengers were not averse to helping the driver by hopping off and giving a push when necessary.

61 Following quickly on the lead taken by Orange Brothers, another north eastern operator, R Armstrong & Sons of Oak Villa Garage, Ebchester, Co Durham, also started a daily London service with similar timings. Running under the name of Majestic Parlour Saloons, the company initially used 24-seater normal control Gilfords, switching later to Duple-bodied AEC Regals. The London terminal agent was a great character in the trade in the person of Harry Tovey with premises at 4 York Road, King's Cross. Next door, at no 6, Orange Brothers had their own booking office and, naturally, a certain amount of rivalry built up, especially so some months later when two more concerns, Phillipson's Stella Motor Coach Service and Hebburn-based J Charlton & Sons, commenced operations on the Newcastle-London route and decided that York Road was also to be their terminus. Although advance booking was always stressed, a number of would-be [ticketless] passengers invariably turned up some twenty minutes or so before departure time, and one could witness amazing scenes as competing booking office staff issued tickets on the pavement whilst drivers put the luggage on the roof rack -- sometimes only to find the traveller had been booked on another company's service, resulting in a further climb up the ladder to retrieve the offending suitcase. This 1928 picture shows a Gilford 166SD of Majestic waiting outside the York Road offices with, behind it, a Strachan-bodied Gilford of Orange loading for the north.

62 Mr J Glenton Friars of Blaydon-on-Tyne was interested in a very special type of fully fronted observation vehicle at the 1927 Olympia Show. Having operated a 2 ton Argyle and a 2½ ton Star in 1919 -- both chassis fitted with not-too-comfortable detachable rear-entrance brake bodies in which passengers faced each other -- he wished to offer really first class travel for his proposed Newcastle-London service. His choice fell on an ADC with bodywork by Short Brothers, the last word in coach construction at the time. It had a Daimler engine in a chassis designed by the one and only Laurence Pomeroy and the luxury body had two passenger compartments with 14 seats in front and six armchair seats in a rear observation saloon, the two sections being separated by a lavatory and a fully equipped kitchen, whilst in the front bulkhead there was an electric fire and a small wine cellar. Three electric fans were also installed. As with other operators, serving of

refreshments was abandoned when it was found passengers preferred to make a brief stop. Originally, when the 12 mph limit was in force, it was intended to serve teas whilst running slowly on a good section of road, but the raising of the limit to 20 mph made a further stop of no consequence to the schedule. The later Daim-

lers of Glenton Friars [Road Coaches] Ltd, though not quite so unconventional, were equally as luxurious in their own way. However, at first it was only leased to Glenton Friars because, as one of a pair [the other was LGOC PR1], the LGOC had a one-year option to purchase, which they declined.

63   Another enterprising concern to attempt to link London with the north east was Galley's, an operator long linked to the Newcastle area, who early in 1928 bought a pair of Karrier 6 wheelers for their new London run although it is now not sure if they operated beyond a Doncaster to Hull service. For a London service this would have been an unwise choice of chassis since the Karrier CL6 was neither fast nor particularly reliable. Davidson's of Trafford Park built the rather bus-like bodies which incorporated rear toilets. Other Great North Road operators not yet mentioned included Cestrian Coaches of Chester-le-Street, F Taylor's Blue Band of Middlesbrough and -- later on -- National Coachways, whose timekeeping was so superb that it was jokingly claimed by the citizens of Middlesbrough that they could set their watches by the National coaches. Some, like Galley, faded under the weight of competition and, sadly, the others, one by one, sold out to the railway and Tilling & BAT-backed United Automobile Services. Charlton's Blue was the last to go in 1935.

64   Competition on the Great North Road was also provided by the London-Scottish coaches. Perhaps the most constantly successful, and certainly amongst the most glamorous of all regular long distance coach operations have been the parallel runs between London and the Scottish cities of Edinburgh and Glasgow. Even today each departure can require several vehicles at the height of the season. The Edinburgh run came first, initiated by Edinburgh pioneer M E Thompson [subsequently Thompson's Tours Ltd] in 1928 as a two-day run, becoming a one-day timing in the following year. Coaches left London's Haymarket at 8am on Tuesdays, Wednesdays and Saturdays, and at the same time southbound from Princes Street on Mondays, Tuesdays and Fridays. The near 400 mile journey was covered in 15 hours, running via Grantham, Doncaster, Newcastle and Coldstream, with fares at 30/- [£1.50] single and 50/- [£2.50] return. Later acquired by Scottish Motor Traction, the service was running both day and night in 1931. Two of SMT's AEC Regals are seen loading in Princes Street in the early thirties in readiness for their 6pm departure on an overnight run to London.

65   Style and luxury in coach bodywork became the keynote of all operators on the lucrative London-Preston/Blackpool run, and this handsome Leyland Tiger of John Bull played its part. Finished in a pleasing two-tone colour scheme, the Blackpool-built Burlingham body had a rear entrance and was fitted with comfortable moquette seating, curtains and a toilet compartment. As one admiring passenger said, when the author 'snapped' the coach in 1931 outside the Central London Coach Station, 'It looked so lovely, I just had to ride in it'. John Bull was the fleet name of Wood Bros [Blackpool] Ltd -- originally registered in August 1920 as J W Dewhurst & Co Ltd, the title being changed in April 1927 -- and appeared on the London road in 1928. Working from the

company's base at 124 Coronation Street, the southbound departure was at 8am and took a route through Lancashire, embracing Blackburn, Darwen and Bolton before joining the A50 to continue by way of Newcastle-under-Lyme and thence through Birmingham and Coventry. The return timing was 8.30am from Bush House, Aldwych. John Bull and its express services to London and Yorkshire, together with tour and excursion operations out of Blackpool, were taken over by the Ribble subsidiary, W C Standerwick, in April 1933.

66 Road-air cooperation. This scene of an Underwood Express Gilford picking up passengers at Onslow Street, Guildford, en route from London to Portsmouth, brings to mind a very small part played by the author in 1932 in introducing a road/air scheme to the Isle of Wight. On one of his infrequent days off, a trip was made to Portsmouth in one of the company's immaculate brown and gold Gilfords, the 8.30am ex Central London Station reaching its destination dead on schedule at 12.35pm, living up to Underwood's slogan of 'Wet or fine, we run to time'. Nearby, an office proclaimed an air service across the water to Ryde operated by the Portsmouth, Southsea & Isle of Wight Aviation Company. The opportunity was too good to miss and, booking a single ticket for 10/- [50p], including car to the airfield, an open cockpit De Havilland biplane was waiting. The flight, which took just 10 minutes, was most exhilarating with wonderful views of Spithead and the Island. The experience was food for thought and after talks with management, the air company and other interested parties, it was decided to publicise through bookings, the airline stating that their new Dragon would be available. During spells of counter duty, the author was able to give first hand details of this novel innovation which was probably one of the very first instances of a coach/air connection.

67 One by one, the major territorial operators wiped most of the smaller independents off the express service map. One such combine company was Crosville Motor Services Ltd, which had been completely reorganised in May 1930 as a wholly owned subsidiary of the LMS Railway and the Tilling & BAT group. A striking addition to the Crosville fleet in 1933 was this 32-seater Leyland-bodied TS4, one of a batch delivered that year. Although destined for the Merseyside-North Wales route they were occasionally put to work as duplicates on the London service. After the war, the vehicles were rebodied as 31-seaters by ECW and were dieselised in 1949. Crosville were well to the fore on the London run with two daily services established by 1929, ex Birkenhead via Stratford-Upon-Avon and ex Liverpool via Coventry, running into the Central London Station as terminal control agents. This was well before Crosville were in the London Coastal fold. The Leylands used in the early days had comfortable red-brown moquette seating [but no toilet facilities] with matching livery of chocolate with the fleet name in large block lettering. All seats were numbered and reserved -- the only long distance service working out of Central London Station which offered that facility. The writer well remembers the regular morning ritual when the two Tigers on the northbound run warmed up for some 5 to 10 minutes before departure. They had been allocated parking positions inside the station with their rear ends against the thin wooden office partition and, consequently, the chartroom was soon filled with acrid exhaust fumes, the staff suffering a most uncomfortable half-hour whilst dealing with the early morning business.

INSIDE STORY

In charabanc days the interior of one vehicle was, perforce, much like that of any other.
And the all-weather gave little scope for the interior designer's art. But as more solid saloon coaches
came into their own, so the trappings of luxury became increasingly prevalent,
the degree of opulence depending on the finance available. Many really sumptuous vehicles were constructed,
different in so many respects from the plastic and glass creations of today.

CURTAINS, mirrors, pillar lights, luggage racks, ashtrays and travelling rugs were all more or less standard fittings, but in many cases small libraries, carpets, chocolate machines, bulkhead clocks and even barometers were fitted. Flower vases were also to be seen, and there was a very proud driver on the ten times daily Cambridge-London service of Varsity Express who ensured that, when possible, a posy of flowers was placed in every wall vase as an added attrac-

tion for his passengers. Being allocated his own vehicle, he spent his stop-over periods between journeys dusting and polishing the handsome two tone blue normal control Gilford as if it was his own private car. Operators were divided on the relative merits of seat covering, but generally moquette upholstery was the most popular with passengers, being warm and inviting as opposed to leather. But moquette presented cleaning problems and those responsible for

68 Lawrence George Hillier of 480-2 Harrow Road, Paddington, favoured patterned moquette for the seating on this Maudslay saloon which was purchased for his daily London-Nottingham service which ran via St Albans, Bedford, Wellingborough, Northampton, Market Harborough, Leicester and Loughborough under the title of Easyway Travel Coaches. The moquette seating adds an air of attraction to a coach that was otherwise in many ways much less sumptuous though more functional than many of its contemporaries. The ceiling covering is particularly plain. An unusual feature is the painted fareboard on the front bulkhead covering the twelve stages on the journey.

preparing vehicles for their next day's journey complained of the difficulty of removing chocolate stains, cigarette ash and, in odd cases, the results of the few passengers who were prone to travel sickness. One operator expressed the view that if leather upholstery was good enough for the private car, then it was good enough for the coach traveller. Owners also differed in their opinion of the necessity for lavatory compartments. Some companies considered the provision of toilet facilities with wash basins, grab handles, paper towels, etc, to be absolutely essential on long distance journeys, whilst others reckoned that a comfort stop every two hours or so was adequate. In theory this may have been so, but in actual practice, valuable time was lost at some stops queueing for facilities and leaving little time to partake of refreshments.

69 Bodybuilders gave considerable thought to interior layout when producing special high class coachwork, as instanced in this sumptuously equipped coach built in 1927. Expressly designed for long distance touring, it was one of a pair supplied to Mr A Warburton of 6 Highbury Lane, Headingley, Leeds, and was built by John Taylor of Barnsley. The ADC 413 chassis had a lengthened wheelbase, enabling an ordinary 32-seater body to be fitted, but the customer stipulated luxury accommodation for only 20 persons. As can be seen, the armchair type seats could be positioned to give a clubroom appearance. These seats had 9ins deep cushion frames with specially sprung backs, and were upholstered in blue antique leather -- and an interesting feature was that each individual swivel seat, designed by Mr Warburton himself, automatically locked itself into position when vacated. The roof interior and side quarter panels were finished in Anaglypta paper tipped with gold leaf, and all window fillets, rails and mouldings were of figured Japanese oak. Other refinements included blue plush curtains, flower vases, clock, bell pushes and bevelled edge mirrors.

70 With the sun roof open, passengers were able to see well above the normal eye level of a closed coach, and trees, sky, mountain tops and tall buildings were all visible without craning necks. This interior aspect of a 1930 Gilford shows the neat foldaway tables in the backs of the leather covered seats, and also the pile carpeted gangway. The fitting of armrests made the seating look compact and comfortable, but this was not always appreciated by the heavier built or larger than average passenger, who preferred to let his figure overlap into the gangway. The woodwork of inlaid mahogany, the casually furled curtains, and the bulkhead clock were more or less mandatory items at the time, and if any criticism at all can be levelled at this particular coach it must be at the paucity of luggage accommodation.

71 A peculiar mixture of contrasts was to be found in a quartet of Leyland PLSC Lions bought by H M S Catherwood in 1927 for his twice-daily Belfast-Dublin express service. Based on the standard Leyland body, they were equipped by Hall Lewis with rather wide, high-backed, leather covered wicker seating for 28 [instead of the usual 35], plus a lavatory in the rear offside corner. These fittings sat uncomfortably in an otherwise standard service bus body complete with its plain matchboard ceiling and lino covered floor. It was, nevertheless, reported at the time that the comfort offered by the new coaches was far superior to that of a third class railway compartment, and with return fares fixed at £1 when the service commenced in the summer of 1927, compared with the rail rate of 26/6 [£1.32½], there was no lack of patronage, especially as light refreshments were supplied on board. Finished in the Catherwood colours of light blue below the waist line and white above, the vehicles covered a daily 208 mile round trip between the two cities.

SOMETHING SPECIAL

True to the pioneering spirit of fifty or more years ago, there was no shortage of operators and manufacturers prepared to gamble on unusual designs and novel fittings irrespective of the extra expense which such special work inevitably caused. Sadly, only in a very few cases did these examples of special enterprise pay off, and it is perhaps as a long-remembered result of the failure of these unconventional designs that the coach industry seldom attempts anything out of the ordinary nowadays.

72 Observation cars have been a phenomenon that has cropped up from time to time over the years. One of the earliest was this 6 cylinder Dorman engined W&G for Gladwyn Parlour Car Services Ltd of Woodhouse Road, Mansfield which, though not all that handsome, was unique for its time. After allowing for a staircase fore and aft, the observation saloon could only have held a very few passengers so its value would have been very limited. The story of coaching in the late twenties is dotted with failures of which Gladwyn was one. The company went into liquidation in May 1929 after failing to make a profit on services such as London-Liverpool, Leeds-Liverpool and Nottingham/Mansfield-London. This 'parlour car' was in a livery of imitation polished wood and off-white.

73 On Tuesday, 14th August 1928 the very first motor coach service in Europe to provide sleeping bunks was inaugurated between London and Liverpool. This was an outstanding development in long distance coach travel and was operated by Albatross Roadways Ltd using an AEC 426 with a pantechnicon-like appearance. The vehicle, designed and built by Phoenix Coachworks Ltd, was powered by the quiet-running Daimler sleeve valve engine and had berths for twelve passengers. Buffet and lavatory compartments were also provided. Initially, Albatross ran three times a week in each direction, but the following year it became a nightly frequency and was re-routed via Manchester. At the same time a new thrice weekly overnight run was instituted between London and Leeds/Bradford. However, the whole enterprise was less than a success and it folded up thirteen months after it started.

74 Some nine months after Albatross had introduced their purpose-built sleeping car to the roads of Britain, another contender entered the running, this time on an overnight London-Manchester run. A concern by the name of Land Liners Ltd of Edgware commissioned bodybuilders Strachan & Brown to construct two fully fronted double deck sleeping coaches on Guy FCX-type six wheeled chassis. Accommodation was provided for 21 passengers in two and four-berth cabins, giving ten bunks on the lower deck whilst, amidships, a straight six-step staircase, placed at right angles across the coach, led from the nearside lower gangway to the upper offside gangway and thence to the remaining bunks on the top deck. A kitchen was located between the two driving axles, and luggage was stored in a compartment in the full width driver's cab. The complete vehicle was 30ft long and 13ft 9ins high. Headroom in the cabins was 5ft 10ins. Like Albatross, Land Liners soon had to retire from the coaching scene, the limited utilisation of sleeper-only coaches working only nine hours out of 24 for six nights a week not being an economical proposition. Certainly Land Liners' night fare of 15/6 [77½p] single or 30/- [£1.50] return [including bed and breakfast] was too low to be a paying proposition.

75 The observation saloon context was taken one stage further by Glenton Friars, whose splendid coaches were acknowledged as providing *the* service on the Great North Road. The culmination of his efforts to provide the maximum of luxury was a number of raised observation Daimler saloons with beautifully constructed, fabric covered bodies by the 1922-established Hoyal Body Corporation. With luxury seating in blue coloured moquette, they had three steps which led from the lower saloon to the twelve seats in the observation section. Ample luggage space was provided at the rear of the coach. Later a batch of nine similar vehicles was purchased by National Coachways -- a new joint venture by Glenton Friars and Frank Lyne of the Central London Coach Station -- also for service on the Great North Road. In 1932 Glenton Friars [Road Coaches] Ltd and National Coachways Ltd were both acquired by United Automobile and the vehicles were repainted in United colours but still carrying their old fleet names. It was sad, in a way, to see the Daimler observations in red and cream livery proudly trying to maintain the former dignity of their once elite operations. United ran them on the Great North Road service for about twelve months -- and then oblivion!

76 Comfort was the keynote of the Daimler observations as exemplified by this interior view of the armchair seating on a National Coachways vehicle. The rear toilet compartment occupied the complete width of the coach. With traffic increasing and with an eye to expansion, the company planned an alternative route between London and Newcastle by acquiring the London-Leeds/Bradford operations of Doncaster-based B&E [Bentinck & Ensign] Motor Services. This concern took the midland road to the West Riding via Northampton, Leicester, Nottingham and Mansfield, and the idea was to extend northwards to Tyneside. This would have given a change of scenery for travellers on a return journey and also opened up quite a few through facilities for inter-mediate passengers - but it was not to be. There were no less than 22 objectors at the subsequent hearing before the Traffic Commissioners, and although no other concern was working such a through route, the application was turned down. Both Frank Lyne and J Glenton Friars realised there was no point in running a business if they were not allowed to expand, and it was for this reason that their coaching interests were sold to United.

77 & 78   A few other operators also dabbled in observation coaches in a small way. One was the South London based Blue Belle Motors, an associate of the Red & White group from 1936, who bought some on AEC Regal chassis for use on their seasonal routes to the coast. One is seen on a refreshment halt during a charter trip. Hardly an idyllic location for a picnic, one might think, but the passengers seem oblivious of the presence of hearby houses as they eat their sandwiches. Dennis Brothers Ltd of Guildford exhibited their version of the observation coach at the 1932 Scottish Motor Show. Based on the economical and very reliable Lancet I chassis, the factory-built body seated 26 persons, and the Lancet's rather cumbersome and ugly front end was offset by the pleasing streamlined appearance. From the author's experience, the travelling public always seemed to appreciate the elevated seats and invariably made a beeline for them first, but even so operators generally remained loathe to invest in what was still considered as unconventional machine.

79   The steady growth of air travel was the most exciting transport development of pre-war years, and it was only natural that airport coach operators should call for that extra something to distinguish their vehicles from the run-of-the-mill coaches in everyday use. Based on a Dennis Ace chassis, this peculiarly shaped airline coach was one of the most exotic of all, and was put into service at Liverpool airport by the Corporation in 1935. Intended to look ultra modern, it appeared rather more like an outsize Dinky toy than a real life coach. Nevertheless, its unusual design gave good publicity to the small, up-and-coming air services from Merseyside as the vehicle ferried passengers to and from Lime Street Station, the Adelphi Hotel and the city's Speke Aerodrome. The war brought a cessation to civilian air passenger services, and the Ace was then converted to more mundane work as a van.

COACH STATIONS

The fast growth of a nationwide express coach network, and the ever-increasing popularity of coastal excursions, brought an inevitable demand for improved terminal and interchange facilities.
Wet and draughty pavements, devoid of any facilities, would no longer suffice and, besides, in several cities the police and other authorities were becoming restive over the congestion alleged to be caused by the on-street parking of express coaches. In this chapter we review a few of the stations built specifically to cater for long distance coach passengers. It is significant to note that few of them are still in existence today.

80 Busy scenes like this became increasingly commonplace in London as yet more companies entered the sphere of long distance coaching. Coach stations were the answer, and although four large ones were in being in the London area by 1931 -- one near Kennington Oval, two in the King's Cross district and the fourth in Lupus Street, Pimlico -- a number of services continued to work into the centre of the capital. Locations such as Regent Street, Southampton Row, Vauxhall Bridge Road and Aldwych were used as terminal points and the resultant congestion became a problem. This picture shows three of the seven 20-seater Reos in the fleet of Mr and Mrs Oliver's Southsea-based Alexandra Motor Coaches Ltd, utilising Buckingham Palace Road, Victoria, as a picking-up point with various other operators' vehicles behind. In 1928, apart from seasonal services, at least seven separate concerns were working the popular London-Portsmouth/ Southsea route originally pioneered by Alexandra. Standardised fares at this time were 7/- [35p] single, 8/6 [42½p] day return and 12/- [60p] period return.

81 Good terminal facilities in London had become of vital importance to the provincial operator and the announcement of the opening of the capital's first covered-in coach station was welcomed by the independents. Ideally situated in Cartwright Gardens, just behind St Pancras Church, with several bus routes just three minutes' walk away and within easy reach of local underground stations, the Central London [Road Transport] Station Ltd was ready to receive coaches in May 1928. Under the able guidance of Frank Lyne, and with space for over forty vehicles, the station initially had a single entrance and exit but a one-way system was soon introduced with the entrance in adjoining Burton Street. Many owners moved their services into the new terminus and one of the first to take advantage of its convenient location was Cambrian Coaches, a large fleet operator running to some fourteen or so coastal destinations. The picture was taken soon after the opening and gives an idea of the traffic being handled. Unfortunately, A M Kemp-Gee Ltd, owners of Cambrian Coaches, went into voluntary liquidation in October 1929, but passengers were not affected as Julius & Lockwood of Lewisham and Thornes of Brixton also worked a full range of coastal services out of the station. The demise of the Cartwright Gardens coach station as such came in 1933 when a new company was formed to concentrate on terminal facilities for goods haulage, but its spirit lives on -- it is now a fleet depôt for the Greater London Council.

82 & 83 The predecessor of today's Victoria Coach Station was in the Pimlico district at 1A Lupus Street. Opened on 1st April 1928, it was actually a very large open piece of ground with a private house at the entrance converted into offices. One could not class the station as easily accessible, being a good ten minutes walk down Vauxhall Bridge Road from Victoria, although six LCC tram routes from south of the Thames stopped some 250 yards away. The terminus was controlled by London Coastal Coaches Ltd, a company formed in April 1925 to act as a centralised booking organisation for the combine companies starting to operate services into the metropolis. The original constituent shareholders were Southdown, United Automobile, East Kent, Maidstone & District, the National Omnibus & Transport Company and Elliott Brothers [Royal Blue] of Bournemouth. By 1929 more territorial companies had established medium or long distance services and they, too, became shareholders in London Coastal; concerns such as Eastern Counties Road Car, Thames Valley, Aldershot & District, Midland Red, East Yorkshire, North Western, South Midland, West Yorkshire, etc. With all these operators using 1A Lupus Street there was a certain amount of congestion at times even though the station had room for 150 vehicles. The picture was taken soon after 9am on a Saturday in June only 2½ months after the terminus had opened. The vehicle on the extreme right is a Gilford in the Aldershot & District fleet, bound for Farnham, standing next to four Southdowns -- three Tilling-Stevens and a Leyland -- in their resplendent green livery, waiting to load for Eastbourne, Brighton, Portsmouth and Little-hampton. In the frontal view of the coach station, a placard affixed to the upper stories gives a clue to the future of the site. It reads 'This site has been secured through the generosity of the public. The frontage has been given as a free gift by the Duke of Westminster. The site will be developed for building houses for Westminster workers'.

84 The London Terminal Coach Station was the third of the capital's big stations to come into operation, opening for traffic in the late summer of 1929. Owned by Coach Travels Ltd, the directors of which also controlled Blue Belle Motors Ltd, it was situated at 80 Clapham Road, SW9, a most valuable site a few minutes walk from the Oval underground. It was claimed to be the largest of its kind in Britain and without any doubt its appearance was most impressive, extending back from the main road some 850 ft. On each side of the open approach were booking offices, waiting rooms, a tea room, buffet bar and shops, whilst the actual covered-in portion had six arrival and departure platforms. Unfortunately, its South London location was a little off the beaten track as far as the centre of London was concerned, and although a fair number of long distance companies like MacShanes of Liverpool, Majestic of Manchester and Bush & Twiddy of Norwich extended their terminus from the West End and King's Cross areas, it was mainly used for South of England services. Blue Belle's large fleet was transferred there from premises at Brixton, using the new station as a basis for their programme of excursions and coastal services. Three of their own AEC Regals are seen preparing for a Saturday morning departure. The terminal coach station was sold to Red & White.

85 Orange Luxury Coaches forestalled the general trend towards the construction of coach stations when, in 1926, they opened their own main station and interchange point at 1 Effra Road, Brixton. Orange had a number of pick-up points in the northern suburbs, together with a secondary base at 45 Parkhurst Road, Holloway, and passengers to and from all coastal destinations would change from their particular feeder coach to the allocated vehicle at either Holloway or Brixton. In this busy view, Guy and Halley all-weathers are seen preparing to depart from Brixton for a variety of south coast resorts. In the winter of 1931, when the author visited Effra Road, not a coach was to be seen. The busy summer station, which proudly flew its own flag from the ramparts, had been temporarily converted into a giant amusement centre and the large arched fascia over the entrance to the covered section had been board over and displayed the words, 'Pleasureland admission free'.

86 Mr H R Lapper joined the Cheltenham-based Black & White Motorways in 1928 and became director and general manager, straight away starting new services in all directions. Expansion was rapid and by 1929 regular schedules were radiating from this Gloucester-shire spa to Cardiff, Southsea, Bournemouth, Weston-Super-Mare, Birmingham, Leicester, etc, and the London frequency had been increased to four departures daily. By offering a wide range of connections at Cheltenham, passengers were able to book through tickets between, say, Bristol and Coventry, Hereford and Portsmouth, or Ludlow and Shaftesbury. To offer adequate interchange facilities, the company opened its coach station in the town which, later on, was to become an important focal point for express services to and from all parts of the country. In this early view at the new station, two of Black & White's Leyland-bodied Tigers are to the forefront. Cloche hats for ladies were essentially a 1920s fashion, but several are still to be seen as their wearers await their departure times.

87 When London's Victoria Coach Station opened for business at the beginning of 1932, all the 26 railway associated companies, together with some half-dozen large independents, moved there from Lupus Street. The changeover was smooth and orderly, with little inconvenience to passengers, as typified in this photo taken on 25th March 1932 of three Eastern Counties vehicles loading for Norwich. The two duplicates at the rear were normally used on local Norfolk services but supplemented the more comfortable express coach at busy periods. The one nearer to the camera is a Tilling-Stevens Express with Short Brothers body and the other is a slightly older United-bodied ADC 423. During the late 1920s the flag of the combine had been borne by United Automobile Services maintaining the Norwich link, but as the result of a reshuffle Eastern Counties Omnibus Company Ltd was formed in 1931 to absorb the original Eastern Counties

Road Car, together with Ortona of Cambridge, Peterborough Electric Traction and the East Anglia services of United Auto.

88 Until 1930 George Ewer & Company's head office was in Leonard Street, Shoreditch, and the coach fleet was garaged in railway arches nearby. Obviously, with increasing expansion, more suitable premises were desirable and a large detached house on a main road in North London was purchased -- 55 Stamford Hill. The house itself became the charting and administrative offices and a booking hall was built on. The back garden was used to build a garage to accommodate some 40 coaches, and the front garden became a fore-court. The transformation at Stamford Hill is shown in this typical Saturday morning scene in 1932, with three Grey Green Leyland Tigers

loading for destinations as far apart as Torquay and Great Yarmouth.

89 In 1935 George Ewer & Co Ltd purchased the goodwill of the East London firm of Plotts & Goldman who served certain coastal resorts under the name of Central London Motors. The firm's coaches were not involved in the acquisition but George Ewer completed the building of a garage at Mile End which Central London Motors had started, and 345 Mile End Road became an important pick-up point for many of Grey Green's services. To carry the overflow of booked passengers at busy weekends, it was frequently necessary to hire a number of extra vehicles, and this pre-war picture taken at the Mile End coach station shows a Leyland Tiger owned by Harris's Coaches of Grays loading for Margate alongside a Gilford of Hounslow-based Hall's Coaches bound for Portsmouth and Southsea.

ACCIDENTS WILL HAPPEN

A highly improbable story, but nevertheless true, is recounted by an ex-Royal Blue inspector.

HARKENING back to the days of the open coach, he was driving towards London when, on rounding a bend, he saw a car on the wrong side of the road overtaking a horse and cart. With the car coming straight at him, the driver took immediate avoiding action by mounting the grass verge, lurching violently into a ditch and, after a few very bumpy yards, managing to regain the road. The car had meanwhile come to grief and our friend dashed back to the scene to render assistance. Returning to the coach, he spotted one of his lady passengers making her way from the adjacent field, and mentioned to her that she should let him know if she wished to leave the vehicle in case she were left behind. The lady explained that she had been dozing on one of the rear seats, and the next she knew she was lying on the grass, having been thrown out when the vehicle tilted into the ditch. Although a little dazed, and sporting a few bruises, she was none the worse for her experience.

89A Even in very recent times serious coaching accidents - resulting in fatalities - have occurred as a result of brake failure, making good headline material in the national press. In the earlier days of coaching the risk was very much greater because the brakes and other security systems were much more primitive. Disaster befell this Maudslay on the last day of October 1920 at Oxenhope when the brakes failed whilst on an outing from Hebden Bridge. The canvas hood, strewn flat along the seat tops, illustrates the complete lack of protection afforded to charabanc passengers in the event of a vehicle overturning.

90 Charabanc outings were not, on occasions, all that tranquil, as the passengers discovered when Sir Douglas Haig came to grief 200 miles from home. The breakdown wagon of the Egham Motor Company was soon in action when this 32-seater needed emergency treatment. The vehicle was owned by the Newton Moor Haulage Co Ltd of Hyde, Cheshire -- a company formed in the Spring of 1919, primarily to carry goods to and from the Manchester district -- and judging by the scars, it presumably toppled over on its near side. No mean achievement with a 12 mph speed limit.

91 A good year for turnover! With much lower speeds than today, and far less traffic, accidents were fortunately a rare event, but nevertheless there were occasions when coaches did come to grief. This mid-twenties picture shows a Shamrock & Rambler all-weather Lancia which suffered the indignity of being photographed on its side. Some operators were extremely conscious of adverse publicity and Royal Blue, for example, issued instructions to its mechanics that, when going to the scene of a mishap, the first thing to do on arrival was to paste plain brown paper over the company's name to hide it from any press cameras.

92 'A funny thing happened to me on the way to the races!' This Gatehouse Coaches Gilford 1680T came off second best in an argument with a loaded wagon when bound for Newmarket, but not all accidents could be attributed to speed or careless driving. There was high unemployment in certain areas in the early 1930s and some drivers were only too willing to do extra turns of duty to gain a few more 'bob'.

Some concerns were sensitive to safety, like Crosville, whose drivers had the third day off after a two-day round trip to London. Others, such as Glenton Friars, carried two men to share the driving on their Tyne-Thames trunk service, but some smaller operators allowed long spells at the wheel without adequate rest. There was an unfortunate instance, just prior to the Road Traffic Act, when a driver, having left his Lancashire base in the morning and arriving in London in the evening, had a short nap in his coach and then returned northwards the same night. He nodded off about 3am through sheer fatigue, and the dozing passengers were treated to an extremely bumpy ride as the vehicle mounted the grass verge. There were no injuries on this occasion but a few weeks later a similar, but more serious accident near Derby in the early hours stopped this practice.

CONTINENTAL INTERLUDE

In the years before World War II, Continental travel was only within the reach of the middle and upper classes. But this did not deter a number of enterprising coach owners from opening up fresh fields beyond the Channel. Air travel was still very much in its infancy, and for those not fancying a long sea voyage, the motor coach presented an increasingly popular alternative to the trans-Europe rail services as a means of organised travel to exotic places.

93   One of the grand old names of the pre-war motor coaching world was Chapman & Sons [Eastbourne] Ltd, who were one of the earliest pioneers of Continental coach touring. Incorporated as a limited company in June 1921, it is recorded that the enterprising William and George Chapman undertook a six-day tour of North Wales as far back as 1910 using a 22-seater Dennis, and in 1919 ran trips to Flanders and the French battlefields, following this up two or three years later with regular overseas tours. With a 50-plus fleet of 14, 22 and 28-seaters, places for excursions and tours were very much in demand, and the yellow liveried vehicles also ran a regular twice-daily summer service between their home base and the capital. Chapman's were acquired by Southdown in 1932, a passing much regretted by regular holidaymakers. The present day Southdown/National coach station and garage in Cavendish Place was previously Chapman's premises, and the photograph shows two of the company's 22-seater Hora-bodied Dennises collecting passengers from hotels in the immediate vicinity of the depôt.

94 & 95 The name of Motorways Ltd was once synonymous with the best in overseas coach travel, the company having commenced as early as 1920 with a service from London to the Mediterranean. From its headquarters at 36 Haymarket, SW1, it set the fashion with tours lasting up to 32 days and reaching out to France, Spain, Germany, Holland, Belgium, Italy, Switzerland, Austria and Czechoslovakia. They also operated a series of home tours, the latter catering mainly for overseas visitors. The company set a standard of vehicle comfort second to none. As a press report stated, following an inspection of one of Motorways' latest coaches, 'The vehicle bears on the road the same relation to a charabanc that the railway Pullman car bears to a crowded excursion train'. A Maudslay 20-seater, delivered for service in 1927, is illustrated and it fully deserved the description of Super-luxury Pullman Saloon. Incorporated in it was an individual armchair for each tourist, a personal luggage trunk, a buffet for teas and light refreshments, toilet, individual glass-topped tables and maps, and 'listening-in' earphones. The interior shot shows the sumptuousness of the four-passenger rear observation compartment, or 'drawing room' as it was termed.

96 Motorways Ltd, whose slogan was *'See Europe from an Armchair'*, were worried about competition from other operators using the word 'Motorways' in their title, and even felt it necessary to advertise that they were in no way connected with various organisations who were flattering them by adopting the Motorways title to distinguish themselves. Examples were Eastern Motorways, Black & White Motorways, Clan Motorways, Lowland Motorways, etc. The firm, under the guidance of its general manager, Graham Lyon, ventured on to the Continent using a couple of ex-US Army truck chassis fitted with specially equipped bodies. The company specialised in tours to North Africa as well as to the continent of Europe. A fleet addition for the 1927 season was this Duple-bodied Berliet which accommodated only ten seats in great comfort. Cane armchair seats were employed, each having a folding glass table in front, whilst at the back of the saloon a miniature buffet was installed, but there was no toilet.

FOR LUXURY TOURING.

97 The accompanying photograph of a buffet compartment at the rear of a Motorways tourer shows just how much could be squeezed into a cramped space. A geyser hot water heater is fixed to the wall and a gas ring is installed, the fuel for which is obtained from a cylinder of compressed gas. The crockery is carried in a special cabinet with racks to prevent the possibility of breakage, and sliding doors, whilst folding shelves and racks are included and are so disposed as to take up very little space when unfolded. The vehicle in this instance is a Strachan & Brown-bodied Dennis of 1925 vintage. For many years Motorways Ltd maintained a reputation for luxury Continental tours and when the concern ceased to exist, a second all-British company was formed under the name of Motorways [1930] Ltd, with an entirely new board of directors and fresh capital and acquiring the goodwill and assets of its predecessors. The new company's fleet in the Spring of 1930 consisted of five Weymann-bodied AECs, one Maudslay and one Berliet.

98 Yet another early operator of overseas services was London-based GB Motor Tours Ltd, who started motor operations in March 1923. At first they concentrated on a most comprehensive series of conducted sightseeing tours for overseas visitors, and later the company worked regular services to Brighton and Eastbourne before branching out on a seasonal London-Brussels schedule. This was not a high class inclusive tour akin to operations like those of Motorways and others, but was more like an extension of the normal internal express coach operations which were rapidly becoming so popular. One of the coaches in the nine-strong fleet allocated to this run is seen outside the offices of the terminal agents, Hickie, Borman Grant & Co Ltd in Cockspur Street. The unusual protruding rear end was a deep luggage compartment and any excess baggage was carried on the roof. Passengers left London at 8am, transferred to the cross-channel boat at Dover and continued in another coach from Ostend to the Belgian capital. The return journey left 35 Rue de Malines at 9am and the overall journey time was about 12 hours. Fares, including 2nd class travel on the steamer, were 34/6 [£1.72½] single and 68/6 [£3.42½] return, with a special weekend return being offered at 56/6 [£2.82½].

COMFORT STOP

A stop at a pub was all part of the outing in leisurely charabanc days but with the coming
of regular long distance services time became important and it was essential that any refreshment halt
or comfort stop should be of limited duration. Initially there was no problem but, as more companies
began to compete with each other on the same road, using the same stops,
then sometimes the standard of service suffered as cafés and restaurants strove to cope with several coaches
arriving at the same time. The Central Tea Rooms at Dunstable, for example, was chosen
by four operators on the London-Blackpool run - Smith & Bracewell, Scout, John Bull
and Standerwick - all leaving the capital at 8.30am and pulling in for coffee within a few minutes
of each other, the rush repeating itself on the southbound journey at teatime. Add, also,
the considerable number of duplicates during the summer peak periods, plus other companies on the A5,
then surely passengers must have felt thankful if their particular vehicle was equipped with
a lavatory compartment. Operators were divided on the merits of this latter facility but a good proportion
of long distance concerns maintained that, to be able to compete with the railways and rival services,
it was necessary to set a high standard and, therefore, in their opinion a toilet section was highly desirable.
So, as early as 1927, vehicles so equipped started to make an appearance. Some operators went a bit farther
and attempted the serving of snacks and refreshments, but these facilities were normally quickly withdrawn
in favour of the roadside café, the coaching world's traditional Comfort Stop.

99 Ensuring the horses were watered first was the maxim for the good four-in-hand coachman when making a refreshment stop, but the custom did not necessarily end with the coming of the mechanical steed. Watched by interested bystanders, this Karrier is having its thirst quenched after the driver and passengers had patronised the adjacent bar. The converted lorry chassis, owned by a Kilmarnock operator, wa on an outing to Girvan on the Ayrshire coast soon after the First War. Not all resorts welcomed the charabanc, however -- Bournemouth, for instance, in the early 1920s tried to stop visiting coaches by insisting that all vehicles entering the town carrying 18 or more passengers should have two drivers. In those post-war happy-go-lucky summers excursionists swarmed to the seaside, not least of all to Blackpool, where the 17 mile stretch of road out of Preston carried a steady stream of charas from Lancashire industrial areas.

100 Allnutt's Café in Baldock's wide main street -- some 36½ miles out of London -- was chosen by many operators working the Great North Road as a convenient first and last refreshment halt. A whole variety of medium and long haul services called there. Arrivals were staggered throughout the day, although, with duplicates at busy periods, the staff were sometimes stretched to the limit and not all passengers were able to enjoy their anticipated cup of tea or coffee after waiting to be served, at the same time having to keep an eye on any queue for the 'little boys and girls' rooms. With the average stop lasting 15-20 minutes, the latter point was a valid argument in favour of lavatory equipped coaches. In this 1931 scene an AEC Regal of Fleetways is on the 9.30am London-Lincoln-Grimsby/Cleethorpes run whilst, facing the camera, a London-bound Gilford of Westminster Coaching Services working the 9.15am, ex Cambridge, stands alongside a Leyland, Middlesbrough bound, in the service of United.

101 The hamlet of Fenny Bridges on the A30 was a morning coffee stop for most of the half dozen or so operators on the eastbound South Devon-London run. Pictured in 1929, the Gilford in the foreground, owned by one Henry L Askew of Chiswick and running as Fleetway, is working the 9.45am ex Torquay service. A couple of hundred yards or so behind the photographer was the hump-back bridge over the River Otter, scene of the well-remembered Superways crash. Very many years later a badly scarred tree still served as a reminder of the crash, and it may be there to this day.

102 In this 1931 setting, passengers on Southern Glideway's 6pm Eastbourne-London service, worked by one of the normal control Gilfords in the company's mixed fleet, stop at Nutley on the A22 for a little liquid refreshment supplied by Tamplins. Not all café and pub owners were glad to serve coach parties. Reg Hele, who for the last thirty years has been enthusiastically guiding the fortunes of Wallace Arnold Tours [Devon] Ltd, whilst reminiscing, showed the writer a 50-year-old letter received by one of the company's predecessors. Dated 1925 and addressed to Ruby Cars from the proprietor of one of the main cafés in Princetown, it stated that he would have to stop the practice of giving free meals to drivers when their coaches stopped for refreshments, as he had recently counted twelve drivers of various companies having a meal in their restroom but only about half-a-dozen passengers eating in the café.

Cafe, Chester

103 The Melbourne Café on the Chester Road at Streetly, Staffs, was another favourite pull-in for express coaches. One of its regular customers was Queen Line Coaches & Baldock Motor Transport Ltd on its daily service between the capital and Llandudno via Coventry, Erdington and Shrewsbury. The Melbourne Café -- situated at the junction of the A452 and B4151 -- provided a convenient midday refreshment halt. Other companies using the road to by-pass Birmingham also stopped there, including Henning Brothers on their London-North Wales run, and at busy periods a marquee had to be erected adjacent to the main café to cater for the many duplicate coaches. A Henning Gilford 1680T and a Queen Line AEC Regal, both London bound, meet at Streetly.

oad, Streetly, Staffs.

The Streamlined Thirties

1930 dawned, and great things were about to happen in the coaching industry. Spurred on by the findings of the Royal Commission on Transport in 1929, the Road Traffic Act was about to come into force, bringing with it the system of road service licensing which we still know today and eliminating the great bulk of competition in all sections of coaching except for private and contract hire.

FROM 1929 the four main line railway companies had been investing heavily in the various territorial undertakings controlled by the combine groups, and under the protection of road service licensing they would be free to pursue a policy of acquiring as many of the small express operators as possible without any fear of others cropping up to take their place. The application of the Road Traffic Act was so harsh that many small operators found themselves in the position of having to withdraw established services, whilst in other cases timings were reduced or intermediate picking-up points eliminated to the extent that profitability could no longer be maintained. In the case of the MT Company's London-Thanet run, for example, intermediate points between Swanley and Birchington -- which the company had served for twelve years -- were barred to it, and it was even prohibited from continuing to pick up at its own established booking office at 322 Vauxhall Bridge Road. In September 1931 *Commercial Motor* reported that up to 30th June of that year 336 applications for licences had been refused by the Traffic Commissioners.

The world economy was in a slump. Bus and coach manufacturers were floundering and in several cases on the

104 The side engined AEC Q-type really gave coachbuilders an opportunity to exploit the possibilities of streamlining to the full. Seen parked in The Square, Bournemouth, this was the first Q-type coach to be built and it went to Elliott Brothers of Bournemouth for service on their Royal Blue South Coast express routes. A flush fitting sliding door behind the nearside front wheel enhanced the smart appearance and, with the back axle located well to the rear of the chassis, the body had a very short overhang. Four Qs were delivered to Royal Blue, two Duple-bodied 35-seaters in 1933, followed the next year by a Harrington 35-seater and another Duple accommodating 37. When this old established and popular operator sold its business to Thomas Tilling Ltd in January 1935, the Qs were not transferred to the Southern and Western National companies to continue on trunk routes but went instead to Hants & Dorset where they were employed for several more years on local tours.

edge of unavoidable collapse. This was the unpromising setting in which the coach industry entered its streamlined era.

105 Prominent amongst the coach body-builders of the period was the firm of London Lorries Ltd of Spring Place, Kentish Town. Designers of the *Plein-Azur* flexible sliding roof, which, it was claimed, could be converted from a parlour saloon to an open coach in only 20 seconds, the company was awarded a Silver Medal at the 1931 Olympia Show, given by the Institute of British Carriage & Automobile Manufacturers. The coach which gained the honour was this 32-seater Lancastria saloon, which clearly showed, in its rounded lines, the dawning of the streamlined era. A Morris Commercial Dictator, it was purchased by Black & White Coaches of Leytonstone, for use on excursion and seasonal coastal services. The goodwill and licences of Black & White [Walthamstow] Ltd -- as the company later became -- together with its subsidiary, Majestic Luxury Coaches Ltd, were bought by George Ewer & Co Ltd in 1956.

---

106 In 1934 Birch Brothers Ltd of Kentish Town designed and built this 35-seater centre entrance coach on a Leyland Lion chassis. Known as the Birch-Airflo, the builders claimed that its practical body lines were based on correct loading and aerodynamic principles and that it was the greatest advance yet in psv coachwork. The full fronted cab gave exceptional driver visibility with the windscreen having a four-bladed Trico Full-Vision wiper, giving a clear rectangular patch 5ft wide by 1ft deep, and the D-shaped appearance allowed an enormous luggage boot above the driver's cab, the contents being retained in position by chromium plated rails and a substantial silken rope. Other features included a fully opening roof, and passengers had the benefit of a concealed wireless located under the front bulkhead clock.

107 The AEC Q was not the only passenger chassis on the mid-thirties market to demand a new approach in body styling. Maudslay's SF40, though retaining the traditional front-located engine, had its front axle set back to allow the entrance door to be placed ahead of it, and this very neat frontal arrangement made a fully fronted body inevitable. It might have been thought that a full front, devoid of the traditional radiator grille, would make for a very characterless vehicle, but this was not so. This pleasant 4 cylinder SF40 was supplied to A P Saunders of Chasetown in his Silent Knight livery in 1936 and had coachwork by Auto-cellulose of Smethwick. The starting handle looks a little out of place on an otherwise very modernistic body.

108 Not all coachbuilders were equally quick to adopt streamlining. Harold J Willett Ltd of Colchester were obviously torn between the old and the new when they built this demons-trator in 1934. A concession to later trends is provided by the curved 'flash' which sits uncomfortably upon a body whose shape is definitely a hangover from the late nineteen twenties. The chassis is a Ford BB type which, despite its very sweet running V8 engine, was never a match for the Bedford range which was now sweeping the market for lightweight coaches. This coach subsequently began its working life with J W Rock of Stourbridge and gave good service to a variety of owners up to 1952.

LUXURY COACH BODIES

109 & 110 Streamlining *par excellence* was the order of the day on this petrol engined AEC Regal for Valliant Direct Coaches. Strachan built the body and included a full width cab even though the Regal was a conventional type chassis, and this full front incorporates a somewhat garish chromium plated grille in place of the manufacturer's handsome radiator. Earlier, in 1933, English Electric had half-heartedly tried to disguise the half-cab on a Standerwick Leyland Tiger by providing a dummy nearside front window following the same outline as the offside of the body. Extremes in streamlining techniques, such as these two vehicles represent in their different ways, fortunately remained the exception to the rule as most operators preferred more conventional lines of development.

111 Diesel power came increasingly to the fore on larger coaches as the decade wore on. Though many of the earlier diesel engines quite definitely lacked finesse and gave a higher level of noise and vibration than their petrol counterparts, their greater economy of operation ensured their growing popularity with many operators. This 1934 vehicle was one of the first Bristol JO5Gs to be built and was supplied to Graham Brothers Ltd of Kirkintilloch, who ran the largest fleet of Bristols in Scotland until they sold out to Alexander in 1938. As anyone who remembers the five cylinder JO5G will confirm, it was far from speedy and, when driven hard, passengers seated near the front were treated to a kind of vibro-massage; altogether an unusual choice of chassis for a luxury coach.

112 Stepped waistrails became a feature favoured by several manufacturers in the middle of the decade. Generally, the rear seats were raised higher than those at the front of the coach for improved visibility, but the effect on the exterior styling was sometimes less than happy. Here a body incorporating this styling feature is seen mounted on a Bedford WTB chassis. The Bedford story is one of miraculously fast growth and it quickly became a firm favourite with operators all over the country following its introduction in 1931, and this 1936 machine is seen in the service of the Highland Transport Co Ltd, a nominally independent concern in which the LMS Railway held a fifty percent interest. It is seen on a typically damp day in Inverness awaiting passengers for a day excursion to misty Loch Maree and Gairloch.

113 When Dennis built the body for this Lancet 32-seater for Blue Saloon of Guildford in 1937 they incorporated a dummy stepped waist-rail without actually raising the level of the rear high backed seats. The high bonnet of this normal control saloon coach makes it a very impressive and powerful looking machine, but such large bonneted models were becoming very much a rarity as operators preferred to opt for the greater seating capacity made possible by the forward control layout. Even more rare, by this time, were vehicles imported from overseas, the demand for which had dried up as home manufacturers provided better coverage of the diminishing market, and by the end of the decade the only foreign name in the list of available models was that of Opel.

114   Crossing the Tyne Bridge at the end of its long haul up the Great North Road, the diesel powered Leyland TS8 Tiger on United's Tyne-Tees-Thames service has a rear entrance Brush body. Destined to spend 18 years with the company, it was the first of a batch of nine similar coaches delivered in 1938. The number plate was originally located just under the windscreen but was later repositioned at the bottom of the radiator by the starting handle, and at the same time the Leyland nameplate on the radiator was replaced by one bearing the United title. When these nine vehicles were renumbered and repainted a little later, they were given the Orange fleet name, continuing to perpetuate the original 1927 pioneer on the London-Newcastle run.

115 In this immediate pre-war scene, set in the little town of Lyndhurst in the New Forest, a couple of wild ponies say 'How do you do?' to the driver of the Morris 8, watched by the passengers of a fully laden Bedford of Shamrock & Rambler as it meanders peacefully along on a half-day trip from Bournemouth. It was in 1924 that Bill Whitelock, son of the company's original founder, linked up with Mr A T E Ransom's Rambler concern and formed Shamrock & Rambler Motor Coaches Ltd. The amalgamated fleet then totalled just five charabancs. Competition even as early as 1924 was quite intense, there being no fewer than 23 coach companies in Bournemouth offering day and half-day excursions. The Duple body on this Bedford WTB has taken one step further in the streamlining process; the roof luggage rack has now been eliminated.

116 In the final year of the decade this fine AEC Regal was put on the road by J Abbott & Sons of Blackpool. If ever there was a classic body design of the era it was Thomas Harrington's Hove-built specimen with distinctive rear dorsal fin. The fin, though theoretically an aid to air circulation within the saloon, was more often than not chosen by purchasers simply because it had style, so much so that it was again very successfully revived when coach construction was resumed after the war. Many fine vehicles such as this saw only a short spell of coach service before being requisitioned for military work with the onset of war.

COACHES GO TO WAR

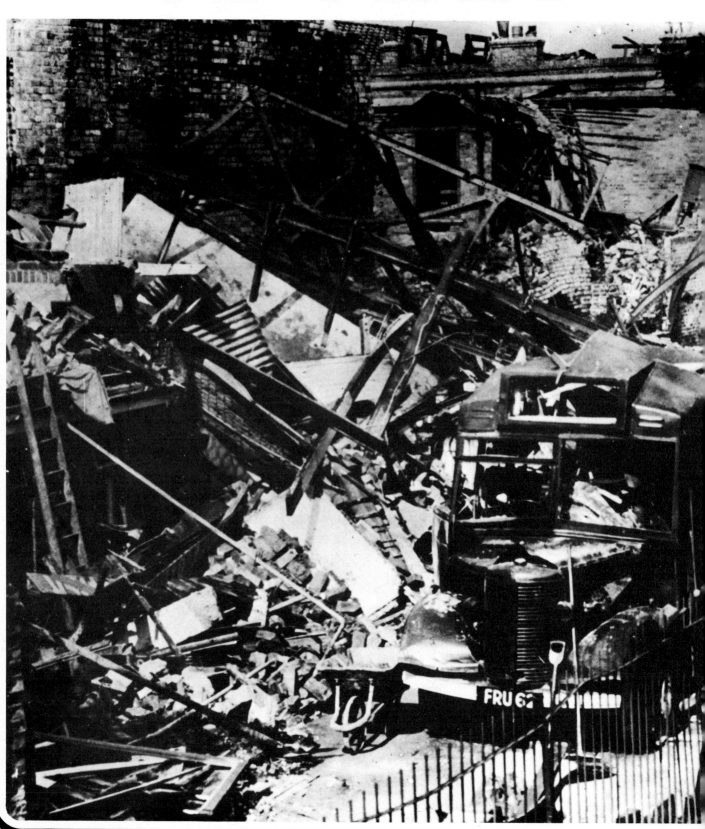

FRU 62

After a busy 1939 summer season, the outbreak of hostilities in September somewhat curtailed pleasure operations and coach owners faced a drastic change in their activities. Express services carried on for some while, albeit on a reduced basis, but the military authorities started visiting garages requisitioning vehicles and, although war needs naturally took top priority, it must have been with mixed feelings that operators saw comparatively new coaches commandeered for use by the Services.

THERE was hardly an operator whose vehicles did not play their full part in the war effort. Luxury coaches of Leeds-based Wallace Arnold, for example, were to be seen crossing the French countryside loaded with troops; they were at Dover for the Dunkirk evacuations and subsequently they travelled all over the north carrying war workers and prisoners of war. It is recorded that during those years the Wallace Arnold fleet covered a mileage equivalent to a journey around the world every other day.

In a much smaller way Sutton's of Clacton 'went to war'. When the company's thrice daily London service was withdrawn, coaches that were not requisitioned were directed to airfield construction work in East Anglia. The drivers who, because of age, were not eligible for call-up stayed with their vehicles to conserve precious fuel and found billets at farms or private houses in the area, returning to Clacton at weekends for vehicle maintenance to be carried out. Petrol was severely rationed and owner George Sutton had to make occasional trips with spare tins of petrol to keep the vehicles on the road.

Many operators' coaches were allocated to Army units stationed in out of the way places and used for general troop transport. The author first sat behind the wheel of an AEC Regal in 1940 and, whilst taking a load of 'the lads' from camp to the baths in Cambridge, wondered which owner's bright livery lay beneath the thick coat of drab khaki which completely obliterated all traces of identity.

117 Many Shamrock & Rambler employees were serving with the Forces, and Doug Ascott, a pre-war driver with the company, recalled a coincidence whilst in France in 1940. Cut off after Dunkirk was finally overrun, he made his way to the Atlantic coast with his unit and, whilst waiting to be evacuated from St Nazaire, he was astounded to see his old coach on the quayside, bullet-ridden and abandoned, having served to the bitter end. At home, his former colleagues were coping with blackout conditions. Managing Director Bill Whitelock, in command of all Shamrock & Rambler units in Bournemouth, needed, at times, to be in touch with his drivers and the military authorities, and on one occasion set off at night for Salisbury Plain. Stopping near an airfield to find his bearings, he was arrested by an alert guard after a search of his car boot revealed ominous pieces of ironmongery. He was released later when it was explained to the officer of the guard that the items were not parts of a secret weapon but spare water pumps and the like for his coaches. Then came the day when Holdenhurst Road depôt was destroyed. On Sunday, 23rd May 1943, a lone enemy plane on a daylight raid scored a direct hit, resulting in two employee casualties and fifteen vehicles being either destroyed or seriously damaged. The least badly damaged ones were extricated and hastily repaired and, though in some cases minus windows or roof, they were running next morning to fulfil essential works contracts. An almost new Bedford 'utility' is seen in ruins.

118 The gay, carefree holiday atmosphere of Shamrock & Rambler's Bournemouth headquarters in Holdenhurst Road was to take on a more sombre aspect during the dark years. The company had some of their fleet purchased outright by the government, whilst other vehicles were directed to a variety of uses. Freshly painted in a grim and forbidding wartime grey, over fifty coaches were under contract for the transport of troops, moving ENSA concert parties from camp to camp, conveying Land Army girls to and from outlying farms, etc. In the May/June 1940 epic of Dunkirk when, in a matter of days, over 224,000 British and 112,000 French and Belgian troops were evacuated, Shamrock & Rambler played its part in company with many other operators, working non-stop day and night carrying the rescued troops from South Coast ports. In the weeks that followed, with Britain under threat of invasion, the company's vehicles were allotted the task of moving army personnel on a dawn and dusk stand-by twice daily to and from likely airborne landing areas on Salisbury Plain, being responsible for the operation of some 120 coaches.

119 Grey Green had pre-war experience in mass movement of personnel, having already carried out such tasks as transporting a contingent of Indian Army troops at the Coronation celebrations in 1937, upon which task a 1931 Leyland Tiger is seen leading the convoy. It was among many in the fleet which later saw active service. The company's East Anglian express services ceased in 1942 for the duration but, well before then, although a number of vehicles had been sold to the War Department, the majority were engaged in carrying workers to and from new camp sites, hospitals, airfields and secret projects. Some jobs were unspectacular but others, like the Mulberry Harbour assignment, involved the complicated conveyance of a large work force. Grey Green was entrusted with large building contracts all over the south and a senior driver was put in charge of each. The Labour Ministry issued priority permits to enable the necessary drivers to be employed, and in between spells of driving, the men were able to help the building constructors.

120 With Union Jacks prominently displayed, and garlanded with patriotic coloured bunting, this Leyland Tiger TS7 in the Lincolnshire Road Car Company's fleet was used in a recruiting campaign during the latter months of 1939 and early 1940. Normally employed on express services [the company first appeared on the Grimsby-London run by the pre-war acquisition of Fleetways Ltd], the vehicle was delivered in April 1935 and worked for 24 years before being sold. The centre entrance luxury Burlingham body accommodated 35 passengers in moquette upholstered seats, and whilst touring the county on behalf of the Services, carried loudspeaker equipment on the roof, with the operator's green livery forming a suitable background for 'Join the Army' posters and other publicity material.

[Right]
122 Wish me luck as you wave me goodbye! Gaunt and strained faces of these early wartime coach travellers barely hide the underlying worries, perhaps of sons and husbands overseas, or perhaps of fear from the ever-present danger from the enemy's bombs for those forced to stay at home. Express coach services were maintained for a while after the outbreak of war and were hard pressed to meet the greatly enhanced demand. In this view at Victoria Coach Station, two fully booked Bristols prepare to leave London on Royal Blue's Bournemouth service.

121   As if motoring were not difficult enough with heavily masked headlamps and blacked-out streets, regular express services that were still running prior to their final withdrawal for the duration encountered further problems when they entered restricted coastal areas. All vehicles were stopped for checking. Concrete blocks, interlocked with embedded iron girders and barbed wire, were stretched across the roads, leaving just sufficient space for coaches and buses to pass through. All passengers had to show identity cards and troops ensured that no member of the fifth column or unauthorised civilians penetrated into no-go zones to witness gun emplacements, mined beaches and other anti-invasion preparations. With road signposts removed to confuse the enemy -- even country railway station identities were obliterated so that German parachute troops could not verify their position -- drivers relied on memory when travelling in the blackout. A Royal Blue Leyland Tiger of 1930, bought secondhand from Devon General and modernised with a new Beadle body in 1936, stops at a roadblock on a 1942 run to Plymouth.

123 In all parts of Britain, operators large and small found their vehicles 'doing their bit' in one way or another. London's Green Line coaches, for example, were turned into ambulances and, likewise, in the West Country, Grey Cars had nine Harrington-bodied Regals, new in 1938, posted to Devonport naval base for ambulance work. The conversion consisted of removing all passenger seats and enlarging the rear luggage compartment to enable stretcher cases to be passed through to specially adapted berths. Persons injured in air raids were moved in these vehicles, and later D-Day casualties were carried.

124 & 125 In the north the large United Automobile Services provided buses and coaches for attachment to army units in Northern Command, with 250 vehicles and drivers standing at the ready day and night to move troops to possible invasion points in Durham, Yorkshire and Northumberland. Two Home Guard motor coach platoons were also formed, each of 58 officers and men, and vehicles were allotted for emergency use. With blacked-out windows, the AEC Reliance originally owned by West Hartlepool-based Eastern Express Motors Ltd and acquired by United in 1930, was converted to an ambulance for the Ministry of Health. Further south, the 1930-built Petty-bodied AJS Pilot -- once the pride of Grays & District Express Motors -- serves with the Auxiliary Fire Service. Obscure makes of vehicle such as this were pretty much a dead loss for wartime work because of the almost total absence of spare parts, and many failed to survive through to peacetime.

126 Although all vulnerable parts of the country were protected by coach-borne troops on a dawn and dusk stand-by basis, it was appreciated that the main threat of any attempted enemy landing would be concentrated in southern areas nearest the Continental ports. Royal Blue, with a large fleet based in Bournemouth, had the task of ferrying the military to and from likely invasion landing points covering a wide expanse of Dorset and Hampshire. This scene shows platoons of infantry disembarking from three Leyland Tigers in the wild heathlands of the area.

127 The war at long last inevitably drew to its end. Throughout the whole horrific episode coaches had fully played their part. On 11th May 1945, three days after the ending of hostilities in Europe, a Duple-bodied Leyland Tiger of SMT delivers German emissaries at Scottish Command headquarters, a converted mansion house near Edinburgh. Rebuilding of the coach industry to meet post-war needs could now commence, but first the headlamp masks and other trappings of war could be quickly removed now that the lights had once again been switched on to celebrate the arrival of peace.

128 Far too many vehicles were wartime casualties, such as this Southern National Bedford/Duple 25-seater. Built in 1936, it had spent the balmy pre-war years on the North Devon coast where it had been allocated to renew the Scarlet Pimpernel fleet acquired in that year. In the early days of the war it was transferred to Swanage by which time it had lost its red Scarlet Pimpernel identity in favour of the standard green and cream of Southern National. The fateful day came on 20th April 1942 when Swanage was bombed and three of the company's vehicles became victims of the air attack, including AOD 873, which also received a shower of machine gun bullets, one of which killed the driver. The damaged coach was moved to Radipole garage, Weymouth, where it remained until after the war and was then repaired by Tiverton Coachbuilders Ltd. It returned to Swanage for further service before finally being sold for scrap in March 1953.

POSTWAR REVIVAL

War was over. The coaching industry quite rightly looked forward to a well-deserved period of stability and it immediately began to gear itself up to meet the anticipated boom in passenger travel. But a cloud loomed on the horizon to herald an unsettled era for the industry. Not the spectre of falling trade, increasing costs and staff shortage -- although these later became real enough problems -- but something more insidious.

IN 1947 the Labour administration passed through Parliament the Transport Act to herald nationalisation of the road passenger transport industry. Coach operators wondered what lay ahead for them. 1948 saw the sale to the British Transport Commission of the vast Tilling organisation, with the SMT and Red & White groups subsequently following suit. Thus much of the express coach network became state owned. However, the government duly changed and nationalisation never

finally spread as far as was once intended, so numerous enterprising independents remained highly active in the excursions, tours, and private hire sectors.

129 Towards the end of 1945 -- shortly after the war finally finished -- the Ministry of War Transport authorised the various traffic commissioners throughout the country to allow the resumption of express services on a limited scale. Shortage of labour and vehicles, plus the time taken to submit applications and for the hearings to take place, meant that a considerable time would elapse before there was anything like a full-scale return to pre-war

standards and it was some four to five months before the trickle started. Tour operators also had to bide their time, but there was a ready market waiting. Six years of war, with its resultant travel restrictions, had forced people to take their holidays at home and now, with more peaceful days ahead, came the urge to find an outlet from austerity. By 1948 extended tours were again being run to Wales, the Lake District, Devon and Cornwall, and Scotland. There was, however, a grave shortage of new coaches, and even on some quite prestigious tours, operators were forced to use obsolete rolling stock. Far from home, an impressive but outmoded Leyland Tigress of Southdown stands in the rain at Inverness bus station on an early post-war Highland tour.

130 Some real relics survived the war, though for most of them their Indian summer lasted only two or three years. Hardly capable of achieving a Highland tour like the Southdown Tigress, this immaculately painted vehicle of George & Leslie was, nevertheless, quite capable of completing a half-day excursion without too much trouble. Standing on the promenade at Southend-on-Sea, with the famous Kursaal and the equally famous gasworks as a back-cloth, this Leyland Lioness, with its canvas roof thrown right open in the summer sunshine, must have seemed very tempting for a 1/9 [8½p] grand tour to Ashingdon, Canewden and Stambridge [stopping for refreshments], or a 2/3 [11½p] jaunt to sample the delights of Creeksea.

131 One of the smartest and finest coaches built in the early post-war years was AEC's Regal III. Ilfracombe, much favoured as a centre by extended tour operators, is the setting for the author's 1949 photo featuring a smart Brush-bodied Regal on a Devon and Cornwall assignment. On the far side of the road a pre-war Bristol of Black & White Motorways stands outside the offices of Southern National/ Royal Blue -- premises originally occupied by Scarlet Pimpernel Coaches, the popular local concern who, in addition to running excursions and tours out of Ilfracombe, once operated a seasonal express service to London.

132 In the boom years following the war, coaches ran with few spare seats. People had more money to spend and were keen to avail themselves of days at the seaside which had not been possible for several years. Fuel was still limited and vehicles had to work hard, but with the private car not a serious competitor and, therefore, traffic congestion not as it is today, vehicles could attain a good daily mileage. The ubiquitous Bedford OB filled many gaps in operators' fleets when larger vehicles were in short supply. Supplied in 27 or 29-seat form and bodied mainly by Duple, they were predominant on many short and medium distance services, and although not in the luxury class, their

simple comfort was appreciated by the travelling public after several years of austerity and restrictions. This vehicle of Bristol-based Wessex Coaches is seen outside the Whiteladies Road depôt picking up passengers for an

afternoon tour, whilst to the rear stands one of the rare, just pre-war Opels which formed an interesting part of the company's fleet for some years.

133   Despite the gradual process of rationalisation that had taken place over the years, coach operators of the nineteen forties still had an almost bewilderingly wide selection of makes from which to choose when placing their orders for new vehicles. Maudslay was doing very well with its Marathon, though few would have guessed, when this Westnor-bodied machine was supplied to a Bath operator, that before long the old established Maudslay concern would wilt away after being acquired as a unit of the Associated Commercial Vehicles combine. This Marathon Mark III had an AEC diesel engine, but some post-war Maudslays were petrol powered, and were the last full-sized British passenger chassis to be thus equipped.

134   Just after the war there was an enormous demand for new coach bodies, not only for building on to new chassis, but also for the renovation of some of the more modern pre-war ones still in existence. Like a flashback to the nineteen twenties, a rash of small coachbuilders

135 Petrol rationing came to an end in 1950 with a consequent build-up in the number of private cars on the road, but at the same time coach travel continued to increase. On 11th February 1950, the Minister of Transport announced that all new four-wheeled public service vehicles registered after 1st June of that year could be up to 30ft in length, and from then on coachbuilders were able to produce bodies giving a greater seating capacity. Larger coaches than hitherto were soon to be seen in operators' fleets, and the wilds of Dartmoor near Widecombe is the setting for this 1956 Plaxton-bodied Commer Avenger 41-seater in the cream livery of Wallace Arnold Tours [Devon] Ltd. This offshoot of the Leeds-based parent came on the South Devon scene in 1947 with the purchase of the Paignton firm of Waverley Motor Coach Tours Ltd and then, with the subsequent acquisition in the following years of Ruby Cars, Devon Touring Company, Excelsior Coach Tours and Cream Cars, it became a formidable competitor to the Grey Cars branch of the BET's Devon General company.

sprang up to fulfil the demand. Most disappeared again just as quickly once the market became saturated. One such organisation was Challenger's of Oldham, whose 1949 advertisement illustrates a sample of their work based on a new Crossley chassis. If its outdated, pre-war styling was typical of Challenger's output, it is no wonder that they failed to make much of a name for themselves in the coaching market.

136 The post-war revival took a depressingly long time to come about. This land fit for heroes still suffered shortages and rationing several years after the war ended. David MacBrayne Ltd, always masters of publicity when it came to promoting their excellent Highland coach tours and steamer services, included this text in their 1952 brochure, which showed how hard life could still be seven years after the war ended. One of their inter-island steamers is depicted and also one of their fleet of Maudslay coaches, which gave many thousands of passengers their first glimpse of the beauties of Scotland's remoter areas.

THE EDGE OF THE WORLD

by

ALASTAIR BORTHWICK

In a world that is still far more troubled than any of us expected it would be so long after the war, the one thing the average man and his wife want is peace. They want to forget form-filling and shortages, half-empty shops and coal doled out by the lump like precious metal. This is especially so when holiday-time comes round. Then, as at no other time, they want to get away—not only from their home, but from worry. The whole of Britain is in that state known to doctors when they say: "You need a change".

In Scotland it is possible to have a change, a much more far-reaching one than a simple transfer of scene. In Scotland you can step clean out of the twentieth century. On our western seaboard there lies a region barely touched by time, where life goes on much as it did hundreds of years ago and wars are sufficiently mellowed to be romantic. It takes more than a world war to upset the tranquillity of the Isles.

The Western Highlands and Islands await your pleasure. Explore them this year.

137 The Dartmoor National Park has much to offer the tourist in the way of historical interest in wild, rugged beauty and quaint 'olde worlde' villages, and it is a 'must' on the sightseeing list of the majority of visitors to England's South West. And what better way to view its charms than sitting relaxed in a comfortable coach seat and allowing the driver to point out places of note and to negotiate the narrow lanes and bridges? Such was the case with this Wallace Arnold 32-seater down from Leeds on an extended tour of Devon. The vehicle, a Leyland Tiger with Duple body, was originally delivered new in 1949 fitted with the traditional half-cab, but was converted to full front by Yeates three years later. Many half-cab coaches were treated to this 'modernisation' process, but in this instance it was not popular with Wallace Arnold drivers who complained that the cab became uncomfortably hot at times.

138 In 1950 coach design changed radically. For the first time since the very earliest days, the front-mounted engine was no longer universally considered sacrosanct; instead the engine was placed under the floor between the axles. The whole floor space was now available for the carriage of passengers, and body designers could let their imaginations run riot in a whole host of new body styles. Almost overnight the traditional half-cab coach became obsolete. One of the most solid of the first generation of underfloor-engined models was the Leyland Royal Tiger, a Duple-bodied example of which is seen on a Cotswolds day tour in the livery of Cronshaw of Hendon.

139 Homeward bound. Convoys of coaches on the overnight runs from London to Edinburgh and Glasgow have been a familiar sight for many years. The war interrupted things, but the post-war revival was quick and decisive. Though the journey time was still in excess of twelve hours, the return fare showed such a saving compared with rail travel that there was never any shortage of customers. In 1951 the two fleets concerned -- SMT on the Edinburgh run and Western to Glasgow -- were renewed with the latest AEC Regal IVs with very comfortable Alexander 30-seater bodies equipped with reclining seats, individual reading lights and toilet compartments. Western's were fairly short-lived on the trunk run, but the larger SMT fleet of Regal IVs lasted on the service for over a decade. Eleven of them make up this SMT convoy seen on Soutra Hill, on the A68 north of Lauder, heading for Edinburgh with an older, half-cab Regal bringing up the rear.

140 In a special pose for the photographer, an AEC Reliance of Black & White Motorways -- by now a member of the BET group -- makes a picturesque sight at Ashton-under-Hill, Worcestershire. A good example of later fifties coachbuilding, the Willowbrook body on this vehicle has a deceptively heavy look about it and exudes a high standard of luxury. Of all the various body styles established by coachbuilders for fitting to underfloor-engined chassis, Willowbrook's was one of the most distinctive, finding favour with several major operators. This vehicle is a far cry from the Black & White Reo of a quarter century earlier, depicted in photograph 51.

141 A startling departure from orthodox seating arrangements was incorporated in the Crellin-Duplex patented half-deck design built firstly by the Lincs Trailer Company and later by Norwich-based Mann Egerton. Illustrated here is the first Mann Egerton-built vehicle, an AEC Regal IV for Ripponden & District Motors Ltd. Although this particular body was mounted on an underfloor-engined chassis, it could be adapted to suit any single deck chassis of either the conventional or underfloor type and was sometimes even found on Foden's famous rear engined model. Up to 50 passengers could be carried, with ample space for luggage, and owing to its low overall height the half-decker was able to travel on roads barred to double deckers due to low bridges. Passengers sat in facing pairs of seats at staggered levels with abundant leg room, and the wide windows gave unrestricted views of the countryside, especially from the upper seats. A number of half-deckers were delivered to operators and although ideally suited for excursions, theatre parties and the like, there was a certain reluctance by some passengers to travel facing backwards on lengthy journeys. It was an extremely expensive body to produce and it only paid its way if the operator could have a full load at all times. The design was also quite unsuitable for stage work, and production was abandoned about 1955.

ABROAD AGAIN

During six years of war many thousands of service personnel had journeyed to distant lands
at the nation's expense, and when normality returned the pre-war jaunt to the Continent seemed
a mundane run-of-the-mill affair. Back in civilian clothes, many much-travelled warriors wished to take
their holidays farther afield and the motor coach played its part, although it was several years
before regular overseas services were established. Today British companies, in conjunction
with their European counterparts, operate regular through routes linking London with Rome, Athens,
Alicante, Moscow, etc. Before this, many proving runs were carried out, but none more exciting
than in 1968 when, in a dramatic journey to test both the vehicle and the feasibility
of a regular coach service to India, a Bournemouth-based Excelsior European Motorways coach,
in cooperation with Ford Motor Co, went to Bombay and back, a distance of 13,897 miles, in only 19 days.
The 37ft Plaxton-bodied Ford R226 with a turbo-charged Ford 360 diesel engine averaged 41.2 mph
and did 11.8 miles to the gallon, using only 9¼ pints of oil in the whole trip. But there's more to the story.
Just 10 days after returning to this country it was chartered by Southern Television to take a film unit
to Bombay to cover the London to Sydney Marathon Rally. By the time it got back the coach had covered
30,000 miles and it was then put to work to cover regular operation on European routes.

142   First to Moscow. In 1928 a Scottish born pioneer, Walter Maitland, dreamt of package holidays and tours for the travel hungry and started local excursions from Bournemouth with just one 20-seater coach. Running under the name of Excelsior Motorways, he catered for local holidaymakers up to the outbreak of war when, like most companies, his small coach fleet was engaged on government contracts. In 1949, with his pre-war visions still uppermost in his mind, the first Scottish tour was operated and in the following year a subsidiary company, Excelsior European Motorways Ltd, was formed and a licence to operate Continental tours .obtained. With Walter's son, Vernon, following in father's footsteps, a keen sense of adventure spurred the Maitland family to travel further afield and to contemplate runs not yet attempted by their competitors. The company claimed they were the first British concern to operate post-war tours to Vienna -- this was in 1956 -- and to Moscow, Warsaw and Prague soon after travel restrictions to the Iron Curtain countries were lifted in the following year. Against the background of Moscow University, history was in the making when this Plaxton-bodied AEC was photographed in 1957.

143 Continental travel was slow to pick up immediately after the war, but by the start of the nineteen fifties more and more people were getting the travel bug and venturing further afield. The all-inclusive coach tour was quickly recognised as being a particularly easy means of reaching new horizons, free from all the little worries of being in a strange land that the driver/courier was paid to take care of. With new coaches at a premium, the acquisition of special vehicles for overseas work was largely out of the question, but by 1951 the West Drayton coachbuilding firm of James Whitson & Co Ltd was building a very stylish deck-and-a-half design which won several prizes in overseas competitions. Seen here is a 39-seater of 1952 just back from winning two silver cups at the Nice Coach Rally. Owned by Salopia Saloon Coaches of Whitchurch, it was based on the characterful if noisy Foden rear engined two stroke chassis.

144 Air travel was a fast expanding business, and as aircraft became larger, so higher capacity coaches were needed to provide town to airport connections. An unusual deck-and-a-half model, embodying a continuous roof line resulting in a very high forward saloon, was produced for British European Airways for operation from Central London to Heathrow, the coaches being operated on its behalf by London Transport. Soon afterwards some very similar vehicles were purchased by Manchester Corporation for airport services at Ringway. Based on Leyland's Royal Tiger chassis, they had 41-seat bodies built by S H Bond Ltd on metal frames supplied by Burlingham.

145 In October 1959, Excelsior made a record-breaking journey from London to Moscow when a Ford Thames/Duple coach covered the 1713 road miles in a running time of 33 hrs 21 mins, giving an average speed of 51.16 mph. The overall time of 44 hrs 57 mins may have been even better but for delays at frontier posts -- 2½ hours to clear East German and Polish customs, and a little over 2 hours at Brest for Russian formalities. Absolute minimum time was allowed for taking on food and fuel -- 17 mins at Hanover, 10 mins at Poznan and down to a bare six minute stop at Minsk. Sustained speed on motorways in Belgium and Germany helped the high average rate of travel. Time was lost on the not so good Polish roads; however, this was compensated by the 628 miles from Brest to Moscow on wide straight roads being covered in 11 hrs 22 mins at an average of 55½ mph. Pictured at the end of its journey, the coach stands in Red Square with St Basil's Cathedral in the background. The chassis used on the record run was a standard Ford product apart from the fitting of special tyres, stiffer springing, an Eaton two speed rear axle and four 28 gallon fuel tanks. The body was fitted out with 20 reclining seats, a toilet compartment and a calor gas stove. Looking for all the world as if he is waiting for his next load of passengers for a half-day excursion from his Bournemouth base, a contemplating 'Jock' Williamson, one of Excelsior's drivers, surveys the scene outside the Kremlin.

146 Another combined operation carried out by Ford and Excelsior European Motorways took place in 1970 and involved a 6000 mile trip to Kabul in Afghanistan, which proved to be one of the most arduous British aircraft recovery missions since the war. The expedition of ten people and two Ford vehicles [the other was a D1500 truck] went out to collect a pre-war Hawker Hind biplane which had been in Afghanistan since 1939. A light bomber and general purpose plane of the 1930s, the Hind was used by the RAF until the outbreak of war and was then taken over by the Royal Afghan Air Force. Destined for the Shuttleworth Collection, it was expected that the homeward journey would last less than a week, but it took four times as long and, by the end, the original team of ten had dwindled to three -- Vernon Maitland of Excelsior and his wife Monica, and truck driver Denis Hills. Trouble began on the return journey when the convoy encountered appalling road conditions in Iran, and then a cholera epidemic in Turkey which closed the Bulgarian border. In the middle of the delay, one of Excelsior's drivers had a severe heart attack and was rushed to the American Hospital in Istanbul; then most of the party returned home by air because of personal responsibilities in England. The three stalwarts remained to look after the aircraft and after a total of three weeks negotiation the convoy obtained clearance into Bulgaria. As Vernon Maitland said, 'I hope I never have to make another trip like that. Driving this massive Ford coach entirely on my own from the Turkish border has been like a Sunday joy ride compared with the miseries and frustrations during the weeks I spent trying to get the vehicles into Bulgaria'.

147 The jet age has arrived. But the economics of coach manufacture have now ruled that the great majority of new town to airport coaches will be basically standard models with only minor modifications for airline use, although BEA's mid sixties purchase of special double deck, trailer towing Routemaster coaches was an exception to this rule. The first line vehicles in the British Overseas Airways Corporation's coach fleet in 1960 were nothing more exotic than Bedford SBs with Duple Vega bodies. One is seen in the airline's standard blue, silver and white livery standing at Heathrow alongside one of its latest Comet 4 jet aircraft.

148 The name of Penn Overland Tours Ltd will be remembered for its marathon overseas coach services of the most ambitious kind. From its Hereford base the company specialised in an overland service between Britain and India travelling through fifteen countries on the way. Much of the clientele consisted of students with time on their hands but not too much money in their pockets. The utmost reliability was required of the vehicles employed on this most strenuous service and, when buying new coaches in 1964, the company selected underfloor-engined Guy Chassis. One, complete with Harrington body and 'Australia' destination board in the window, is seen about to board the Dover-Dunkirk ferry on its maiden trip to India. The deep, straight window line and the roof luggage boot combine to give the vehicle something of a Continental look.

THE
MOTORWAY AGE

The opening of the first short section of motorway in 1958 brought the exciting prospect of fast inter-city non-stop coach services within the realms of possibility. Up till then coach travel had, of necessity, been a leisurely and comparatively slow form of passenger transport, but operators were planning ahead for the day when much faster timings could be introduced whilst the railways looked on with little relish at the thought of what this invigorated competition might do to the receipts on their main inter-city runs.

49 For the motorway era, Preston-based Ribble and its offshoot W C Standerwick ordered a batch of rear engined Leyland Atlanteans fitted with double deck coach bodies built by the MCW organisation but designed by Ribble. Intended for long distance services between Lancashire and London, Scotland, the Lake District and the West of England, the big innovation was the serving of refreshments en route by uniformed hostesses -- a revival of the buffet facilities offered by some independents in the late 1920s. Appropriately named *Gay Hostess*, the first coach to be received from the builders represented the company when Ernest Marples, the then Minister of Transport, opened the second section of the M1 motorway to Crick on 2nd November 1959. It is seen here after the ceremony on its way to London -- but not in service.

150 With 30ft as the then permitted maximum length for public service vehicles, the double deck coaches were claimed by Ribble to be unique inasmuch as they were the only coaches of their kind in the world. The new styling incorporated reclining seats, individual reading lights, a toilet compartment and a public address system. Luxury seating was provided for 16 passengers in the lower saloon and 34 in the upper saloon, with most of the seats having adjustable footrests. The chassis had special springing and was fitted with air suspension at the front, although this was later removed. Fifteen of these *Gay Hostess* vehicles entered service with Ribble in 1959/60 whilst 22 similar vehicles joined the Standerwick fleet. The double deckers operated between Blackpool and London for the first time on Tuesday, 31st May 1960, and as each successive stage of the motorway was opened so the journey time was reduced. In 1973, for instance, the fastest Standerwick timing between London and Preston was 4 hrs 55 mins, and to Blackpool 5 hrs 40 mins. A far cry from the advertised schedule of 1932 of just over 11 hrs. In an off-season shot, one of the *Gay Hostess* Atlanteans is seen loading up in an almost deserted Blackpool coach station.

151 Midland Red was also represented on that auspicious November 1959 occasion and actually commenced a Birmingham-London motorway service on the very day the M1 was opened. 807 HHA -- seen at the Digbeth terminus before starting its non-stop run -- was one of a batch of integrally constructed vehicles built in the company's central works in 1959. Classed as CM5T, it was a development of their C5 class coach but fitted additionally with a turbocharger and a special gearbox and over-drive. A lavatory compartment was added and this reduced the passenger capacity to 34 from the standard 37 seats. From 2nd November 1959 the motorway service enabled the journey to be completed in 3 hrs 25 mins, compared with over five hours previously, and nowadays -- with motorways stretching over much of the total distance -- the city to city schedule occupies only 2¼ hours. The CM5T coaches were impressively fast; they could cruise at a steady 80 mph and often reached 85 mph or more. Alas, the 70 mph speed limit on motor-ways has since put paid to such hair-raising journeys.

152 A notable break away from traditional coach design came in 1962 with the Bedford VAL. Three axle coaches had all but died out before the war, and who would have ever dreamt that a six wheeler would come on the market in a big way once again? But this time the twin axles were at the front, whereas in days gone by they had mostly been at the rear. The three axles allowed the load to be spread more evenly, and the smaller wheels gave a lower floor. There was also said to be greater safety in the event of a tyre blow-out but -- until it was cured later on in the production run -- the braking system on the multi-wheeled layout was less than trouble free. Many operators favoured the VAL and its production continued right through to 1972. Who knows whether there will ever again be a multi-axle coach on the British market? Illustrated here is a 1967 VAL with Duple Vega Major body in the huge Grey Green fleet.

153 All plastic laminates and glass! The modern coach interior is bright and cheerful -- as if to match the faces of the smiling ladies on this well-packed hen party excursion -- and long gone are the days when the smells of disinfectant and wax polish greeted the nostrils of the coach traveller. But the feeling of cosy luxury has vanished with the leather and inlaid mahogany in the search for lightness, ease of maintenance and maximum visibility, and this is perhaps a shame. The coach seen here is a Duple Super Vega of the early 1960s.

154 The Anglo-Scottish coach services also benefitted greatly from massive road improvement schemes, notably on the A1 and A74, and through the construction of the M1 and M6 motorways. Coaches no 7 and 11 of a Western SMT overnight contingent to Glasgow are seen at Victoria Coach Station in London on an August day in 1963. Both are Leyland Leopards, the new one on the right being constructed to the latest permissible length of 36ft, which enabled larger passenger loads than ever before to be carried. It carries a stylish Alexander-built Y type body, a design which must surely rank as one of the classics of all time, being still in production little modified seventeen years later on.

155 Towards the end of 1968, Ribble/ Standerwick exhaustively tested a new version of their motorway double decker on the high speed track at the Motor Industry Research Association's proving ground near Nuneaton. The chassis chosen was a Leyland engined Bristol VRL/LH with an 18ft 6ins wheelbase and a stepped-down rear axle to give a lower floor height. Other features included power assisted steering, five speed semi-automatic transmission and a Tecalemit Airdromic mileage controlled automatic lubricator. The body, again designed by Ribble's engineering department, was of all-aluminium alloy semi-integral construction and built in the Lowestoft factory of Eastern Coach Works. It carried 60 people, eighteen in the lower saloon and 42 on the top deck. The toilet compartment with wash basin, illuminated mirror and shaver point was retained but, unlike the *Gay Hostesses*, the new coach was not equipped for the serving of refreshments. A full height luggage compartment with storage racks, giving a capacity of 240 cu ft, was located at the rear of the lower saloon. A fleet of these Bristol VRs duly replaced the *Gay Hostess* Atlanteans but were never as successful as had been hoped, mechanical unreliability contributing to their early downfall.

156 Far removed from any motorways, the Scottish Highlands have retained a growing popularity with British and overseas tourists despite the massive growth of cheap package tours by air to overseas destinations which has hit coach tour operators and hoteliers alike. On the pier at Fort William in June 1971 stands a Highland Omnibuses coach scheduled to take a pre-booked party to see the grandest of wild beauty spots. No youngster, this Duple-bodied AEC Reliance has only recently received the red and blue livery of the Scottish Bus Group subsidiary, having been acquired with the services of David MacBrayne Ltd as part of an early 1970s rationalisation of public transport in the highlands and islands.

157 Successive Transport Acts of 1947, 1962 and 1968 have created, in turn, the British Transport Commission, the Transport Holding Company and the National Bus Company, each presumably being considered necessary to correct the defects and deficiencies of its predecessor. The National Bus Company absorbed into the publicly owned sector the many large bus companies formerly in the private enterprise British Electric Traction group. For a few years most of the former BET companies remained outwardly much as they had been. Some, such as Southdown, Midland Red and Ribble, had built up highly successful programmes of extended tours with a nucleus of faithful clientele, who journeyed with them year after year. A Ribble Plaxton-bodied Leyland Leopard is seen taking its rest at Kyleakin on an Isle of Skye tour while its passengers partake of lunch at a nearby hotel.

158 In 1972 the National Bus Company imposed its corporate image policy on all its subsidiaries. Coaches had to be painted in an uninspired 'livery' of ghostly overall white with the name *National* emblazoned on each side in alternate letters of red and blue. A concession to the parent company's name was that it was carried in smaller letters elsewhere on the coach, but this was little consolation for the loss of long respected, traditional liveries. And so it was that we came to have white Midland Reds, white Royal Blues and white Black & Whites! One surely unforeseen result of this policy was that, at the large coach stations such as Victoria and Cheltenham, it became very difficult to find the right coach at busy times. In the spacious coach station at Paris Street, Exeter, the new and traditional Royal Blue liveries are seen on a couple of Bristol coaches. The rear engined RELH with white painted Plaxton body is of 1971 vintage; the ECW-bodied MW is ten years its senior.

159 The motorway coach services between London and Scotland have been extended in the nineteen seventies -- such has been their success thanks to motorway scheduling -- that two more Scottish Bus Group concerns, Fife and Northern, began sharing in their operation. In 1976 all vehicles received a new corporate *Scottish* livery in white and blue and prominently displaying the cross of St Andrew. This patriotic livery is as bright and distinctive as National's is colourless and insipid, and it illustrates what can be achieved with sound design. Purpose built for long distance, sustained motorway work, the fleet of 12 metre coaches, with bodywork by Alexander, can be found on three makes of chassis: Bristol, Leyland and Volvo. The one illustrated is a Bristol REMH6G in the fleet of Eastern Scottish [the successor to SMT]. Its striking features are the small high set windows, so reminiscent of Trailways and Greyhound vehicles in the USA, and the interior decor and comfort which are up to a very high standard. The four companies now offer no fewer than eleven day and night regular timetable departures in each direction during the summer months, plus many duplicates. These link London direct with Aberdeen via the M1, M6 and M74 in 12¼ hrs; Kirkcaldy is scheduled in 12½ hrs, the fastest timing to Edinburgh takes 10 hrs, whilst an amazing overnight run between the capital and Glasgow can be made in 8½ hrs.

160 In recent years the coach industry has paralleled the motor car market in buying foreign, though to a lesser degree. The great diminution in the number of chassis and body makes available on the home market, coupled with the decline in reliability of many of the more recent models and troubles in spare parts supply, has all combined to induce coach buyers to look across the Channel or to Scandinavia for their new purchases. Volvo has done particularly well with its B58, Mercedes Benz and DAF have made healthy strides, and others are expecting to do well in future. And in recent years coach passengers have become accustomed to the squarer lines and more garish paintwork of coach bodies built in Portugal, Spain, Belgium and elsewhere. Typifying the inroads made by the overseas manufacturers is this Van Hool-bodied Volvo in the service of a very old established British operator, Harris' Coaches of Grays.

INDEX OF PHOTOGRAPHS

Photos have kindly been supplied by:- Ken Blacker; BL Heritage Ltd; Geoff Lumb; London Transport; Prince Marshall; *Motor Transport*; Michael Sutcliffe; Chris Taylor.

First edition copyright Marshall Harris & Baldwin Ltd 1980
ISBN 0 906116 02 3

Published by: Marshall Harris & Baldwin Ltd.
17 Air Street
London, W.1.
Registered in London 1410311
Designed by Brian Harris and Mark Slade
Printed in the United Kingdom by Morrison & Gibb, Edinburgh.